A New Understanding of Poverty

A New Understanding of Poverty

Poverty Measurement and Policy Implications

KRISTIAN NIEMIETZ

The Institute of Economic Affairs

First published in Great Britain in 2011 by
The Institute of Economic Affairs
2 Lord North Street
Westminster
London SW1P 3LB
in association with Profile Books Ltd

The mission of the Institute of Economic Affairs is to improve public understanding of the fundamental institutions of a free society, with particular reference to the role of markets in solving economic and social problems.

ISBN 978 0 255 36638 0

Many IEA publications are translated into languages other than English or are reprinted. Permission to translate or to reprint should be sought from the Director General at the address above.

Typeset in Stone by MacGuru Ltd
info@macguru.org.uk

Printed and bound in Britain by Hobbs the Printers

CONTENTS

THE AUTHOR

Kristian Niemietz is the IEA's Poverty Research Fellow. He is also a PhD student in Public Policy, and a tutor in Economics, at King's College London.

Kristian studied Economics at the Humboldt Universität zu Berlin and the Universidad de Salamanca. He graduated as *Diplom-Volkswirt* (MSc in Economics) in 2007, with a thesis on the privatised pension system in Chile. After graduating, he went on to work for the Berlin-based Institute for Free Enterprise (IUF).

AUTHOR'S ACKNOWLEDGEMENTS

I would like to thank Dr John Meadowcroft for his extremely valuable feedback and suggestions at various stages of writing this monograph.

FOREWORD

When the early poverty researchers Charles Booth and Benjamin Seebohm Rowntree visited the East End of London in the late nineteenth century, they found large numbers of people living in the most desperate poverty: inadequate food and shelter and insanitary conditions were commonplace. For Booth, Rowntree and their contemporaries, measuring poverty was a relatively simple matter of counting the number of people engaged in a daily struggle to exist in the face of absolute hardship.

Today, measuring poverty in developed nations has become a much more complex and contested matter. The struggle to acquire the basic essentials of food, shelter and hygienic conditions no longer exists on such a widespread basis – indeed, it may be argued it no longer exists at all in this country. But many people – including the UK government and charities such as Oxfam and the Child Poverty Action Group – believe that poverty remains rife in the UK. According to some figures, for example, the UK has higher rates of child poverty than Hungary, the Czech Republic and Poland.

What has changed from the late nineteenth to the early twentieth century is the way that poverty is defined and measured. The early poverty researchers measured poverty in absolute terms, while contemporary researchers define poverty relatively. The question that then arises is which measure is the most reliable indicator of the 'real' level of poverty?

In this superb study Kristian Niemietz, a PhD candidate at King's College London and Poverty Research Fellow at the Institute of Economic Affairs, does not dismiss absolute or relative measures of poverty. Rather, he sets out the strengths and weaknesses of both: absolute measures illuminate the kind of hardships described by Booth and Rowntree, but tell us little about the relative deprivations that may prevent people from enjoying what most of their contemporaries would consider a decent life. Relative measures, on the other hand, provide information about people's ability to live what most of their contemporaries consider a decent life, but may mislead if they are assumed to measure absolute physical hardships like those described by the early poverty researchers.

Both absolute and relative measures may inform and mislead. A particular danger is that absolute and relative measures may become confused in the minds of the public and politicians – often descriptions of absolute physical hardship are used to illustrate the existence of relative poverty. In such circumstances policy-makers may produce incoherent and counterproductive policy responses.

Niemietz's solution is a new measure of poverty that takes into account both absolute and relative factors: the Consensual Budget Standard Approach (CBSA). Niemietz's CBSA aims to reflect the social and cultural dimensions of poverty by using survey evidence indicating what a majority of the population consider to be the necessities required to live a decent life. This list of necessities is then converted into a consumption basket and the real cost of this consumption basket then becomes the poverty line used to measure the existence of poverty. Niemietz's approach, then, neatly combines the strengths of both absolute and relative measures while seeking to avoid the defects of both.

Once an effective definition and measure of poverty has been established, then the question of how poverty may be ameliorated can be addressed. Here, Niemietz proposes a number of positive policy solutions set in the context of the fact that economic growth remains the most effective long-term method of poverty reduction. This is not, of course, necessarily the case if the government is trying to reduce poverty defined in the relative sense.

In this monograph Kristian Niemietz demonstrates a deep appreciation of the underlying logic of absolute and relative measures of poverty that has enabled him to show how the strengths of each can be captured in a new single measure. He then goes on to thoughtfully address how the poverty uncovered by a CBSA might be remedied. This outstanding work should be essential reading for all those interested in how poverty should be defined and measured in the second decade of the 21st century and what solutions might then be forthcoming.

JOHN MEADOWCROFT
Lecturer in Public Policy
King's College London
December 2010

The views expressed in this Research Monograph are, as in all IEA publications, those of the author and not those of the Institute (which has no corporate view), its managing trustees, Academic Advisory Council members or senior staff.

SUMMARY

- The impression we obtain about the prevalence of poverty, its time trend, its risk factors and remedies, depends largely on how we define and measure poverty. The choice of a poverty measure is not merely a technical detail; it sets terms of debate and shapes policy.
- The most widely used poverty measures today are 'relative poverty' measures. These do not measure physical deprivation, but lack of income relative to others. Using these measures, the living standards of all people in a society may rise while measured poverty may increase!
- The use of relative benchmarks has been taken further in recent publications such as *The Spirit Level*, which assert that all material consumption beyond a minimum level is completely useless in itself, serving no purpose other than to signal social status. But the way in which these authors draw on the literature on 'subjective well-being' is extremely selective.
- Evidence suggests that the income level that people need in order to participate in a given society in a dignified manner is affected by the incomes of others. However, the relevant reference groups are not simply the inhabitants of the national territory. Reference groups typically consist of people with similar socioeconomic characteristics. The income the

poor need to participate in society in a dignified way will also depend on a number of other factors (such as changing technology and the prices of particular goods and services).

- All income-based poverty measures are flawed in various ways. These flaws arise from, amongst other sources, benefit under-reporting, temporary income fluctuations, differences in access to benefits in kind, and regional price differences. Expenditure data lead to quite a different story about the development of poverty in recent decades.

- Most current poverty measures, whether relative or absolute, unduly direct the policy focus on the nominal incomes of those at the lower end of the income distribution. They divert policy attention away from much simpler and cheaper policy options of poverty amelioration, such as relaxing supply-side constraints in key product markets.

- People widely disagree when asked, in abstract terms, what constitutes poverty. But when asked, more tangibly, what is truly necessary to lead a decent life, there is a more robust consensus. A poverty measure should be based on the ability to purchase goods and services that it is widely believed are necessary to lead a decent life. This would automatically incorporate information about relevant developments in product markets.

- Flawed poverty measures lead to serious policy failures in the arena of tax and benefit reform.

- A realistic poverty measure would point to policy solutions such as the reform of the tax and benefit system to include benefit simplification; the removal of penalties on family formation; low benefit withdrawal rates; and a full-time work requirement for in-work benefits.

- The single most important reforms would be supply-side reforms such as the thorough liberalisation of the land-use planning system. This would enable greater labour mobility and a lower cost of housing. Supply-side reforms would improve the material conditions of the least well-off, not only directly but through many different channels.

TABLES AND FIGURES

A New Understanding of Poverty

1 INTRODUCTION

'The belief that poverty has been virtually eliminated in
Britain is commonly held.'

Peter Townsend (1962)

'It is now almost universally accepted that ... mass poverty
has re-emerged.'

Richard Pryke (1995)

The most well-known early attempts to systematically measure
poverty in Britain are based on the research of Charles Booth
and Benjamin Seebohm Rowntree in the late nineteenth century.
'Poverty', to these researchers, meant a lack of resources necessary to fulfil essential physical needs, such as nutrition, shelter
and clothing, to an adequate standard. Their poverty lines corre-
sponded to the cost of consumption baskets containing basic
'necessities'.[1] Against this yardstick, they compared the living
conditions they observed in the slums of London (Booth) and
York (Rowntree).

Rowntree's research notebooks tell a depressing tale of dirty,
overcrowded backyard dwellings plagued by illness, damp, mould
and cold:

---

1   Booth never explained where his 'line of poverty' came from. But Gillie (1996)
     observes a striking similarity to the income threshold which the London School
     Board used to grant needs-based school fee bursary schemes. The latter was
     based on the cost of a basket of necessities. Gillie demonstrates that Booth was in
     close contact with the London School Board.

No. 33. Field labourer. Married. Two rooms. Two children, school age or under. Very dirty and untidy. Seven houses in this yard, and one water tap. There are supposed to be two closets, but one of these is blocked with deposit and filth, and has been unusable for some time; the stench is unbearable ...

No. 46. Labourer. Married. Four Rooms. Three children, school age or under. Has great trouble. Two children have died, and constant illness in the house. ...

No. 52. Monthly nurse. One room. The last three tenants have been 'carried out' (i.e. died). The ash pits and closets belonging to four other houses adjoin the back wall of the house, and rats and other vermin are common. (Rowntree, 1922: 51–3)

Poverty, at that time, meant unhygienic housing conditions, a stingy diet, insufficient protection from the weather and vulnerability to income shocks. The documents make an even gloomier read when bearing in mind that even these precarious conditions must have represented a considerable improvement, compared with what poverty meant just decades before Rowntree (see Nardinelli, n.d.).

In the first half of the twentieth century, a number of researchers carried out local poverty studies based on Rowntree's basket-of-necessities concept (see Horton and Gregory, 2009: 1–6; Pichaud and Webb, 2004: 33–47; Linsley and Linsley, 1993). While these studies cannot be aggregated into a national average, they convey a rough-and-ready impression of the evolution of poverty during that period. At the turn of the century, poverty was still widespread. But during times of economic expansion, it generally fell. While the early 1930s witnessed a rebound, even the depression could not completely unravel the advances that had been made in the meantime. Rowntree's second study, carried out in 1936, found a working-class poverty rate of 31.1 per cent. But by then he had made considerable amendments to his poverty indicator, which, though still very minimalist by today's standards, was no longer limited to the appalling conditions described above. Abject poverty, in the sense of Rowntree's original indicator, had fallen by well over half.

By the early 1950s, it seemed that the country was finally leaving poverty behind. With only 4 per cent of the adult population able to afford a television, and only 3 per cent a foreign holiday (Marr, 2007: 85), living standards were certainly spartan by present-day standards. But the worst was over. In 1950, Rowntree, now 80 years old, conducted his last study of working-class poverty in York. Using a similar measure as in 1936, the 1950 survey found the working-class poverty rate to be down to 2.8 per cent. This would correspond to less than 2 per cent of the total population.

The optimistic interpretation that poverty had finally been conquered spread quickly. Newspapers cheered the 'end of poverty' (Hatton and Bailey, 2000: 517). The topic disappeared from political manifestos, because it was generally considered no longer important (Glennerster, 2004). For the same reason, academic interest in poverty faded: not a single Rowntree-style poverty study was conducted after 1950 (Hatton and Bailey, 2000: 518). Peter Townsend, who was to become the leading poverty researcher, summarised the situation: 'the belief that poverty has been virtually eliminated in Britain is commonly held' (Townsend, 1962: 210).

Rowntree's figures from the 1950 survey have later been

qualified. Poverty, even by these ascetic standards, had *not* disappeared by 1950 (Hatton and Bailey, 2000: 530). The relevant finding from Rowntree's studies was not the *level*, however, but the *trend* they revealed, which was that of a steady decline in poverty amid generally rising prosperity. The declaration of victory over poverty was premature. But the message that economic progress, combined with a limited safety net, can eventually overcome poverty was powerful.

Paradoxically, a generation later, poverty was back again. The 1960s had already seen a renewed academic interest in the topic, which was later labelled the 'rediscovery of poverty'. At least by the 1990s, the topic had made a full-blown comeback in the public debate. Today, according to Oxfam Great Britain, 'nearly 13 million people live in poverty in the UK – that's 1 in 5 of the population. 3.8 million children in the UK are living in poverty. 2.2 million pensioners in the UK are living in poverty. 7.2 million working age adults in the UK are living in poverty.'[2] End Child Poverty, an umbrella organisation uniting over 150 charities and NGOs, notes that 'the proportion of children living in poverty grew from 1 in 10 in 1979 to 1 in 3 in 1998. Today, 30 per cent of children in Britain are living in poverty.'[3] In an England-wide survey by Ipsos MORI (2006), people were asked about their position on the statement 'There is no such thing as poverty in Britain'. Only 8 per cent agreed. Summarising this phenomenon, Pryke (1995: 13) notes: 'It is now almost universally accepted that … mass poverty has re-emerged.'

The path from the 'end of poverty' to the 'rediscovery of poverty', and finally to the 're-emergence of mass poverty', has to

2   http://www.oxfam.org.uk/resources/ukpoverty/povertyfacts.html.

3   http://www.endchildpoverty.org.uk/why-end-child-poverty/key-facts.

be seen in the light of a fundamental change in the way poverty is commonly understood and measured. What Booth and Rowntree had in mind was poverty in the sense of impeded physical functioning. In the wake of the 'rediscovery of poverty', this understanding was replaced by one of impeded social participation. It was argued that when people's resources fell seriously short of average levels in their society, they would find themselves excluded from customary social activities and lifestyles. They were thus poor, even if their command over goods and services would be considered comfortable in a different setting. This understanding came to be translated into a relative measurement, in which the poverty line was set as a fixed fraction of contemporary average incomes.

As Part I of this monograph will show, the implications of the change have been profound. Had Rowntree's understanding remained prevalent, the above interpretation could not have emerged. Further rounds of Rowntree-style surveys, even with a much broader understanding of what constitutes a 'necessity', would have shown a further decline in poverty. A Rowntree-style measure could only have shown a resurgence of poverty if there had been a pronounced fall in real incomes towards the bottom of the distribution, which did not occur. Real incomes at the bottom have been rising over most of the period.

Had there been no change in the measurement of poverty, the mainstream interpretation today would be that poverty as a social phenomenon disappeared for good during the 1960s or thereabouts. 'Poverty', today, would be seen as a phenomenon affecting specific vulnerable groups such as the homeless – perhaps suffering from addiction or mental health problems. It would not be expressed as a percentage of the population, and it would not

Figure 1 **The evolution of real incomes of the 5th, 10th and 15th percentiles in the UK**
1961–2008 (2008 prices)

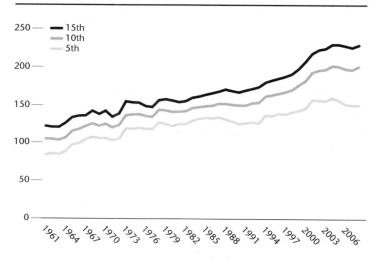

Source: Statistics from Institute for Fiscal Studies (2010)

be thought possible to address this problem within the framework of traditional social policies (since these are precisely the groups beyond the reach of the traditional safety net).

According to Osamu (2007), this is the situation in Japan, where poverty is still commonly understood in a 'Rowntreean' sense. Osamu conducted a large-scale attitude survey in Japan and found that most respondents associated poverty with their country's immediate post-war years, with contemporary developing countries and sometimes with homeless people. Hardly anybody associated the term with low-income groups in present-day Japan.

The vast majority of Osamu's respondents believed that, apart from the mentioned vulnerable groups, poverty no longer existed in Japan.

The comparison between Britain in the 1950s and Britain today, or between Britain today and Japan today, highlights a general property of poverty research: the impression we obtain about the extent, severity, time trend, geographical concentration, risk factors and effective remedies of poverty largely depends on what we mean by 'poverty' in the first place. The measurement of poverty is thus by no means a mere technical detail. The effect, or perceived effect, on the situation of the least well-off individuals in society often acts as a litmus test of economic and social policies. Welfare reforms, labour market reforms, tax reforms and indeed economic and social models as a whole are frequently judged by what they achieve for the least fortunate. As Meyer and Sullivan (2007: 1) put it: 'the change in poverty is relied upon as an indicator of success or failure of our economic system and government policies'.

In the UK today, this indicator is generally the relative measure of poverty. As will be shown below, it has become the preferred measure of most poverty researchers, government departments, the major political parties, vociferous anti-poverty advocacy groups and international organisations such as the EU and UNICEF. The British Social Attitude Survey shows that when asked explicitly, only a minority of the general population approves of the concept. But a relative poverty count is seldom quoted as 'the number of people earning less than 60% of the equivalised median income'. It is reported as 'the number of people falling below the poverty line', or simply as 'the number of people living in poverty'. The language of the poverty debate seems to be designed to obscure rather than illuminate a proper understanding of the issue.

Part I of this monograph shows how the dominance of the relative measure of poverty has shaped the poverty debate. On this measure, the enormous potential of a free economy to raise the living standards of the unfortunate counts for nothing. Activist income policies appear to be the sole determinant of national poverty rates. The relative measure conveys a clear narrative: poverty is low in some countries because their governments keep it low; and high in other countries because their governments tolerate it. This is the impression communicated, for example, by poverty studies from the EU (see Eurostat, 2005a and 2006) and UNICEF (2005, 2007) and also by, for example, a recent publication by the Fabian Society (Horton and Gregory, 2009). The authors write at length about the evolution of poverty in Britain over the twentieth century, without once referring to the dramatic changes in low earners' housing conditions, nutrition, clothing, ability to travel, access to information and communication technology, and ability to buy goods and services related to leisure, culture and recreation.

On the other hand, liberal authors have often rejected relative poverty as just another measure of inequality. They have largely ignored the arguments that gave rise to the relative understanding of poverty and have emphasised the notion that a rising tide lifts all boats, and that a relatively small piece of a big cake can be more tolerable than a relatively big piece of a small one (e.g. Lomasky and Swan, 2009). In purely statistical terms, they are right. Relative poverty is a measure of income inequality in the bottom half of the income distribution. Figure 2 plots the evolution of relative poverty in the UK against the evolution of inequality in

Figure 2   **Inequality versus relative poverty in the UK**
             1961–2008

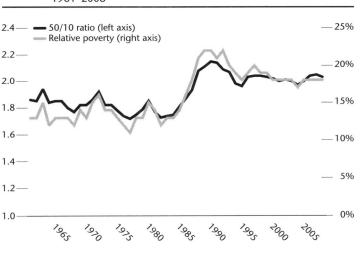

Source: Based on data from Institute for Fiscal Studies (2010)

the bottom half, measured by the ratio of median incomes to incomes at the 10th percentile (P50/P10).

The two measures are indeed easily substituted for one another. This does not, however, necessarily invalidate the arguments underlying the relative measure. Defenders of the relative poverty concept have a valid point: poverty is not absolute, because 'needs' are context specific. Hence, Rowntree-style measures were abandoned for good reason. However widely the views on what precisely constitutes poverty may diverge, there is virtual unanimity that, in the context of modern Britain, amenities such as an indoor bathroom, electricity, hot running water or a fridge are key necessities. A spartan poverty standard that did not cover these items would be seen as irrelevant: it would not resonate with most people's understanding of what constitutes poverty. Yet there is nothing in the nature of the above-mentioned goods that makes them necessities, and most people would not have considered them so three generations ago. The reason why they constitute necessities for us is simply that we live in a society where nearly everybody has these amenities, or, in other words, because overall living standards today are so much higher than three generations ago. And this is precisely the notion which underpins relative measures. Their merit is that they attempt to operationalise the fact that there is nothing 'obvious' or 'objective' about our understanding of what is necessary to live a decent life. These perceptions are related to the overall level of economic development. If a contemporary low earner struggles to pay their electricity bill without overdrawing their bank account, they will not find consolation in knowing that low earners in Rowntree's days had neither electricity nor bank accounts. Nor will a comparison with sub-Saharan Africa be of much relevance. Low earners in contemporary Britain do not live in Rowntree's days, nor in sub-Saharan Africa. They live in a setting in which 'needs' are different. Any refutation of the relative concept has to address these concerns, instead of just reverting to a rising-tide/bigger-pie rhetoric. This is what this present monograph sets out to do.

The conventional growth-versus-redistribution debate also misses the point in other respects, as Part II of this monograph will show. In the medium term, the living standards of the least well-off are heavily affected by developments in product markets which are not reflected in income or expenditure data. A contemporary example is the development of a 'no-frills' market segment in the airline industry and its expansion over the past decade. This development has not just enlarged the air travel market, but shifted its composition in favour of low-income groups. Similar changes can be observed in the supermarket sector and in some markets for consumer electronics. But, as the ongoing debate over 'affordable housing' shows, there are also sectors where no comparable changes have occurred. Most conventional poverty indicators, relative and absolute alike, are blind to enterprise-based pro-poor developments. Perhaps as a consequence, the question of why these occur in some markets but not in others barely appears in the poverty debate. The debate focuses unduly on nominal incomes, which is unfortunate because it precludes potentially effective anti-poverty strategies which come at no fiscal cost. Part II of this monograph will finish with a proposal for a consensual poverty measure which avoids these blind spots.

Part III of this monograph will show how a focus on misleading poverty indicators in the UK has led to flawed anti-poverty policies in the recent past. This is most visible in the design of tax credits. These were originally a tool to improve work incentives and build up earnings capacities, but when employed to this end, their impact on income-based poverty figures will be limited. Some people will not respond to the incentives provided; many of those who do would not have fallen below the poverty line anyway; and the build-up of earnings capacities will take some time either way. When the policy aim is to promote employment, this is not a problem. When the aim is to reach an income-based poverty target within a short time span, it is. This conflict of objectives may explain why the tax credit model adopted in the UK became a confused hybrid model. In raising employment and lowering income poverty, it was at best partially effective, while the fiscal cost was huge. Tax credits are just one example of structural deficiencies in the tax and benefit system.

A more realistic poverty indicator would also facilitate the formulation of more effective and efficient anti-poverty policies. These would rely, to a much greater extent, on people's own capacities to improve their situation, and on the removal of adverse incentives.

PART I: HOW TO MEASURE POVERTY AND WHY IT MATTERS

2 HOW TO MEASURE POVERTY

What is poverty? In research covering the world's least developed countries (LDCs), that question is relatively uncontroversial. It is the inability to afford a minimum standard of goods necessary for physical sustenance, such as food, clothing, shelter and medicine. The most common measure of poverty in LDCs, the $1-a-day standard (which refers to the value of the dollar in the mid-1980s), was originally proposed on the grounds that it broadly corresponded to a minimum quantity of these core necessities (see Ravallion et al., 1991). It was also found to approximate many domestically used poverty lines.

But such a concept of poverty is applicable only up to a certain level of economic development. Poverty as measured against the $1-a-day standard falls steeply as GDP per capita rises (see Figure 3). It rarely occurs at all beyond average income levels of roughly $15,000, which corresponds to the present situation of middle-income countries such as Chile and Malaysia.

World Bank poverty standards such as the $1.25 or $2-a-day standard raise the critical GDP threshold beyond which poverty begins to fade out, but they all show the same tendency. At very low levels of economic development, the question of what is meant by poverty is uncontroversial, and so is the obvious conclusion that in order to fight poverty, these countries have to enable economic growth. Of the six economies shown in Figure 4, Haiti

Figure 3   **$1-a-day poverty versus per-capita-GDP PPP, 116 countries**
2009 or closest available year

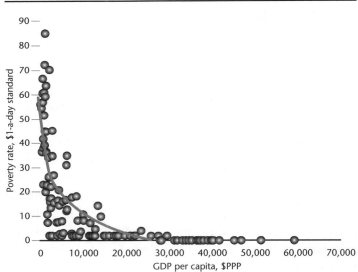

Source: Based on data from CIA (2009) and World Bank (2006)

and Nicaragua have followed low-growth trajectories over the past half-century and display high levels of subsistence poverty. Hong Kong and Singapore have followed high-growth trajectories and have long since left subsistence poverty behind. South Korea and Chile have eventually switched from low-growth to high-growth trajectories, but since their take-offs started later, they have taken longer to grow out of subsistence poverty.

In the contemporary developed world, however, 'poverty' in this most basic, subsistence-related sense disappeared long ago.

Figure 4 **Different growth paths: real GDP per capita in six countries 1961–2008, in international Geary-Khamis dollars of 1990**

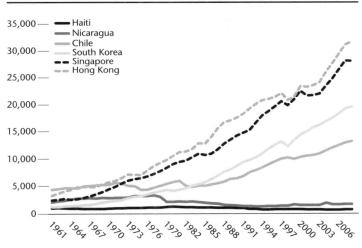

Source: Based on data from Maddison (n.d.)

The British Social Attitudes Survey shows that the *term* 'poverty' may still evoke connotations of a struggle for subsistence (see Sefton, 2009) – but this is not what the poverty indicators commonly applied to developed countries attempt to measure. They attempt to approximate a different underlying concept: one related to social participation, or the ability to comply with the social customs prevailing at a particular time and place.

The underlying concept of poverty involved in this case is therefore much more abstract. Rowntree's indicator could rely, for a good part, on highly tangible measures. The food component of his indicator attempted to reflect a consensus among nutrition scientists on what constituted a minimum nutrient intake for a healthy diet (Rowntree, 1922: 88–106). A similar reasoning was behind the $1-a-day poverty line. There can be no similar consensus on what constitutes 'social participation'. It is this lack of tangible measures which makes poverty research covering the developed world much more sensitive to arbitrary choices. As Kenworthy et al. (2009: 3) put it: 'Once societies move past subsistence levels, there is no non-arbitrary "minimal" standard of living.'

The most common approaches to measuring poverty in the developed world include indicators of relative poverty (RP), subjective poverty (SP), absolute poverty (AP) and material deprivation (MD). Within each of these approaches, there can be substantial differences depending on the precise specification of the indicator.

Relative poverty

Indicators of relative poverty are based on a country's income distribution. Incomes are equivalised, which is the process of making them comparable across different household types. A particular household type, normally a two-adult household, is set as the reference category. For any household type other than the reference category, equivalised income is not the nominal income that a household receives, but the income which a two-adult household would require to attain the same living standard. If a single household's nominal income is £X, then their equivalised income is 1.63*£X (under the so-called McClements equivalence scale), because a single household earning £X and a two-adult household earning 1.63*£X are assumed to achieve the same living standard.

Equivalence weights reflect economies of scale in household consumption, resulting from the shared use of resources such as housing space and household appliances. There are several equivalence scales, which differ in their assumption about the extent of economies of scale within a household and how they relate to the age of a household member. The appropriateness of equivalence scales is a matter of debate. Saunders (2009: 8–9) has criticised equivalence scales for ascribing arbitrary values to different household members. In contrast, Blackburn (1998: 461–2) complements a cross-country poverty analysis with a sensitivity analysis changing the equivalence scale and finds that it has no substantial impact on the results for most countries.

A relative poverty line is a fixed fraction of the central tendency of the income distribution. Thus, households are considered poor if their income is far below those of 'typical' income of a particular time and place. In earlier studies relying on a relative measure, the poverty line was usually set at 50 per cent of mean income (Atkinson, 1998: 2), with 60 per cent of median income later becoming the more common measure. Poverty lines based on the mean can be highly sensitive to a small number of very high incomes, which makes them less suitable to approximate 'typical' incomes (Saunders and Smeeding, 2002: 1–4). On the other hand, the median can be subject to other statistical biases: Easton (2002: 6–7) points out that income redistribution from median to upper-income earners would give the impression of falling poverty.

The poverty rate, or headcount measure, can be complemented by a measure of how far below the poverty line the poor are. Sen's (1976) 'Poverty Gap', the percentage point distance between the average income among the poor population and the poverty line, is a measure of the depth of poverty. It mitigates the

Figure 5   **P50/P10 ratio versus relative poverty, all OECD-countries**
            Mid-2000s

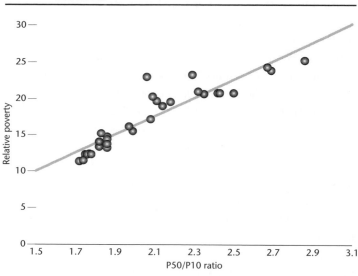

Source: Based on data from OECD (2008)

reliance on an arbitrary cut-off point, by capturing movements below the threshold and not just across it. An alternative consists of looking at a range of poverty thresholds instead of a single one – for example by adding an upper bound and a lower bound.

Statistically, relative poverty is a measure of inequality in the bottom half of the income distribution. The ratio of median incomes to incomes at the 10th percentile, the most common measure of inequality in the lower half of the distribution, largely contains the same information. It is therefore, as Figure 5 shows, the closest correlate of relative poverty measures.

Absolute poverty

Indicators of absolute poverty (AP) are characterised by poverty lines that represent a fixed level of purchasing power, or command over material resources. Two individuals whose incomes are equal to the poverty line always enjoy the same material living standard. The poverty line is not connected to average living standards, so the poverty status of a given individual does not depend on the incomes of others around them.

An absolute poverty line can refer to a living standard which is interpreted, by some criterion, as an 'objective' minimum standard. In this case, there would be some rationale as to why a living standard below this threshold ought to be considered as 'poverty' and a living standard above it should not. The already-mentioned Budget Standard Approach (BSA) pioneered by Seebohm Rowntree falls into this category. The BSA poverty line has an explicit meaning: it is the cost of a preselected consumption basket. A similar logic applies to the World Bank's $1-a-day standard.

In research pertaining to contemporary developed countries, absolute poverty lines seldom have a clear interpretation. They can be derived from simply taking the (relative) poverty line of one particular year, keeping it fixed in real terms, and applying it to subsequent years (see Office for National Statistics & Department for Work and Pensions, 2009a: 41–53; OECD, 2008: 129–30). Or the poverty line can be 'borrowed' from one country and applied to others, adjusting for differences in price levels but not for differences in average incomes (Smeeding, 2006; Notten and Neubourg, 2007). In both cases, the absolute poverty line has no interpretation of its own. Such absolute poverty measures, which are 'borrowed' from a particular country and/or year, and frozen in real terms, will subsequently be called 'quasi-absolute'.

Absolute poverty is sometimes used as a synonym for 'extreme poverty' (Brady, 2003a: 8–10; European Commission, 2004; Picket and Wilkinson, 2007: 6; New Policy Institute & Joseph Rowntree Foundation, n.d.), which is incorrect. The absolute/relative distinction contains no information about the severity of the poverty concept examined. Several authors have used a purchasing-power-parity-adjusted fixed poverty line to compare poverty rates across OECD countries (Scruggs and Allan, 2006; Smeeding, 2006; Notten and Neubourg, 2007). In the less wealthy OECD countries, such as Portugal and Greece, absolute poverty rates of this type can easily be higher than relative rates. Understanding 'absolute poverty' as 'extreme poverty', and 'relative poverty' as 'moderate poverty', confounds two distinct categories. An absolute poverty indicator need not be minimalistic and a relative poverty indicator need not be encompassing.[1]

Absolute poverty measures also approximate living standards by income, or, less frequently, expenditure. Like relative poverty measures, they equivalise income through the use of weighting scales. Poverty gap or composite measures can be derived in the same way as for relative poverty.

Subjective poverty

Subjective poverty indices attempt to overcome the arbitrariness of absolute and relative poverty lines by deriving poverty lines directly from large-scale surveys.

Subjective poverty can mean that each individual assesses their poverty status themselves. People would simply be classified

---

1   The Canadian 'Market-Based Measure', compiled by Statistics Canada, is one of the (very rare) examples of a generous absolute poverty measure.

as poor when they consider themselves so. In this version of subjective poverty, there is no poverty line and no equivalisation. Households can be asked to classify themselves as, for example, 'poor' or 'very poor', which would be a loose equivalent to the poverty gap measure.

The second version of subjective poverty is that of a 'majoritarian' or 'democratic' poverty line. Income and self-assessed poverty status are plotted against one another, to check whether there is a point of inflection in the income distribution below which most respondents consider themselves poor and above which most consider themselves not poor. This inflection point is then used as a poverty line, and respondents are classified accordingly by their income. Alternatively, respondents can be asked directly what they consider to be the necessary minimum income to maintain a minimum decent standard of living in their country. The average of these responses then becomes the poverty line. When done separately for different household types, no equivalisation is required. Poverty gaps can be derived in the same way as for relative and absolute poverty. The majoritarian subjective poverty approach classifies all respondents by the common standard they have collectively agreed upon, whereas under self-assessed subjective poverty, each respondent sets his or her own standards.

Material deprivation

Material deprivation refers to a class of indicators which attempt to measure involuntary lack of 'essential' goods and services. They are based on a predefined consumption basket. Respondents are asked whether they lack any of these items, and whether this is because they cannot afford them or because they do not want the item.

The items can be given different weights – for example, the lack of an item can be judged to be more severe when many other respondents possess it. The 'deprivation score' is the weighted or unweighted number of missing items. The poverty line is set in terms of a deprivation score, not as a monetary value. The average deprivation score among the poor is a kind of poverty gap measure.

Material deprivation indicators differ from Rowntree's Budget Standard Approach insofar as they rely on people's self-assessment, instead of an observable measure of living standards such as income. Table 1 summarises key features of poverty concepts.

Table 1 **Characteristics of common poverty measures**

	Proxy measure of living standards	Poverty line	Proxy measure of the depth of poverty
Relative poverty	Income or expenditure	Fixed fraction of central tendency	Poverty gap
Absolute poverty	Income or expenditure	Fixed real income level	Poverty gap
Subjective poverty (majoritarian)	Income or expenditure	Majority decision	Poverty gap
Subjective poverty (self-assessed)	Self-assessed	–	Self-assessed
Material deprivation	Consumption/ possession of goods and services	Fixed number of missing consumption items	Average deprivation score among the poor

There are alternative ways to classify poverty measures. Boarini and d'Ercole (2006: 11–12) distinguish between 'input-based' and 'outcome-based' measures. The former concentrate on indirect, observable measures of living standards, such as income or expenditure. The latter attempt to measure living standards more directly. Differences can occur when 'inputs' such as income do not directly translate into living standards. Two households may have identical incomes, but may differ in other, unobserved variables that still make them end up with very different living standards. Special health needs leading to high medical expenses, or access to an informal exchange network, would be realistic examples.

Using the categorisation of Boarini and d'Ercole, relative poverty, absolute poverty and majoritarian subjective poverty would count as input-based measures, while material deprivation and self-assessed subjective poverty are outcome-based measures. No information is required on *how* a household manages to obtain all the items in the material deprivation consumption basket, or on *why* a respondent does not consider himself poor.

3 THE MEASURE MATTERS

The choice of the poverty measure is much more than just a technical detail. In one insightful study, Bradshaw and Finch (2003) measure poverty in Britain in 1999 in three different ways: by applying relative poverty, subjective poverty and material deprivation indicators to the same data. All three indicators produce comparable poverty rates (between 17 and 20 per cent). But the relatively poor, the subjectively poor and the materially deprived are not the same people: 'These results indicate a considerable lack of overlap between measures that have been, and still are, used to represent poverty. If the measures were completely uncorrelated one would expect to obtain a distribution that is quite close to the one obtained' (ibid.: 516).

Crucially, each indicator identifies different risk groups, and therefore provides different policy recommendations. Pensioners, for example, are identified as a high-risk group by the relative poverty index, and as a low-risk group by the material deprivation index. The only risk factors which are consistent across all three indicators are obvious ones such as economic inactivity.

In a similar study for Australia, Marks (2007) measures poverty in three different ways. These are relative poverty, subjective poverty and 'financial stress' (a measure of whether people regularly incur arrears on important bills or have to borrow money). Again, the three measures identify three different poverty populations, and the relatively poor, the subjectively poor and the financially stressed are seldom the same people. Only about a third of the relatively poor also experience financial stress; and only around a third of those who feel poor have incomes that fall below the relative poverty line. Unsurprisingly, the indicators also differ in the risk factors they identify. Controlled for other factors, higher education levels are significantly associated with a lower risk of relative income poverty, but not of subjective poverty or financial stress. The risk of financial stress significantly decreases with age, which is not true for the risk of subjective poverty and relative income poverty.

Brewer et al. (2008a: 70–79) measure poverty among families with children in Britain in 2006, first in the sense of relative poverty and then in the sense of material deprivation. Again, the poverty count is roughly similar across both indicators – but only about half of those in relative income poverty are also materially deprived, and vice versa. Further, people with identical incomes can differ vastly in their material deprivation score. The authors regress poverty rates against a set of potential explanatory variables to identify risk factors. Again, apart from obvious candidates such as worklessness, both measures point to different risk factors. The geographical distribution, for example, differs: households living in London are less likely to be in relative income poverty than households with similar characteristics living elsewhere, but more likely to be materially deprived. In Wales, Scotland or Northern Ireland, the opposite is true, certainly a reflection of the large regional differences in the cost of living. Both measures also differ in the household types and the ethnic groups they identify as especially prone to poverty.

Einasto (2002) finds similar discrepancies across poverty

measures for Estonia, where he measures poverty defined as relative poverty, subjective poverty and material deprivation. Less than half of the relatively poor are also materially deprived and vice versa, while only about a third of either group consider themselves poor. Time trends also differ, even over the short period from the mid- to late 1990s.

The same pattern is repeated in cross-country studies. Boarini and d'Ercole (2006) review previous studies using both relative poverty and material deprivation measures; they conclude that the mismatch between the two indicators is a consistent finding across the literature. More recent OECD data shows that on average only about a fifth of those who count as materially deprived also find themselves in relative income poverty (OECD, 2008: 189–93). The correlates of poverty are also different across the two indicators.

Eurostat (2009a) uses a different material deprivation indicator and also finds that when comparing material deprivation with relative poverty in Europe, 'these figures confirm that deprivation and poverty are not concentrated on the same subpopulations and that the relationship between income poverty and deprivation is weaker than could be expected' (ibid.: 9–13).

Van den Bosch et al. (1993) compare relative and subjective poverty rates in seven European regions and small countries. The impression that is obtained about where poverty is concentrated in Europe depends a lot on the choice of indicator. Belgium and the Netherlands, for example, record similar relative poverty rates, but the share of people who consider themselves poor is more than twice as high in Belgium. Again, risk groups differ across indicators (ibid.: 248–53).

These findings are even more pronounced when applied on

a greater scale. The picture of where poverty is geographically concentrated in Europe depends almost entirely on the choice of indicator. Matcovic et al. (2007) show that relative poverty is about as large in western Europe as it is in eastern Europe, with an average rate of about 15 per cent in both regions. Subjective poverty, however, is largely concentrated in eastern Europe, with a discrepancy in poverty rates of 30 percentage points between the EU-15 and the new member states. Subjective poverty exceeds relative poverty in each of the new member states, while the opposite is true in each of the EU-15 states except Greece. A plausible explanation is eastern Europeans' exposure to western European living standards.

Differences such as those described above are no less striking when measuring poverty in relative and in absolute terms and comparing the results. Blackburn (1998: 460), for example, applies a common poverty line – the official poverty line of the USA – to eleven western European and North American nations, adjusting for differences in price levels. The resulting poverty rates differ sharply from the respective relative rates. When plotting relative and absolute rates against one another, a negative correlation is obtained. The most notable outlier is the USA itself, with its extremely high relative and its moderate absolute poverty rate. The author notes that 'poverty comparisons can be very sensitive to whether a relative or absolute standard is used' (ibid.: 450). The study refers, however, to data from the 1980s. The discrepancy has evened out since then, because absolute poverty in the USA has been stagnant while it has fallen further in western Europe.

A similar comparison has been performed by Scruggs and Allan (2006), who also apply a common poverty line – the real equivalent of 40 per cent of the US median income in 1986 – to sixteen OECD countries. Again, absolute and relative rates differ sharply: plotting them against one another produces a negative correlation. The two countries that have recorded the greatest increase in relative poverty over the period observed here, Ireland and the Netherlands, are also the ones which recorded the largest decrease in absolute poverty!

Notten and De Neubourg (2007) as well as Smeeding (2006) also apply the purchasing-power-parity-converted US poverty line with western Europe and North America. Contrary to the above authors, these studies do find that relative poverty and absolute poverty are correlated when taking a cross-country snapshot for the year 2000. But they also find that time trends differ strongly across indicators. The discrepancy is particularly strong for Ireland and Spain, which simultaneously record pronounced falls in absolute poverty and increases in relative poverty.

Such discrepancies are unsurprising when looking at the changes in the underlying real incomes. Table 2 ranks five selected countries by their percentage point change in relative poverty between the mid-1990s and the mid-2000s. It also shows annual changes in real incomes at the bottom and in the middle of the distribution, since relative poverty rates rise when incomes towards the bottom of the distribution rise more slowly than median incomes (Spain, Ireland), or fall faster (Turkey). Relative poverty falls when incomes towards the bottom of the distribution rise faster than median incomes (France), or fall more slowly (Mexico).

Table 2 **Changes in real incomes and in relative poverty rates, selected countries, mid-1990s to mid-2000s**

	Annual % change in real incomes of the bottom quintile	Annual % change in real median incomes	Cumulative change in the relative poverty rate (percentage points)
Mexico	−0.1	−0.2	−3.3
France	+0.9	+0.8	−0.4
Turkey	−1.1	−0.3	+1.4
Spain	+5.2	+5.5	+1.9
Ireland	+5.2	+8.2	+4.4

Source: Statistics from OECD (2008)

Table 3 shows that such patterns have also occurred in the UK over time.

Table 3 **Changes in real incomes and in relative poverty rates, UK, selected five-year periods**

Five-year period	Annual % change in real incomes of the 10th percentile	Annual % change in real median incomes	Cumulative change in the relative poverty rate (percentage points)
1973–77	−0.4	−1.8	−2.3
1978–82	−0.4	−0.6	−0.8
1961–65	+2.4	+2.4	+0.1
1995–99	+2.0	+2.8	+1.3
1983–87	+1.0	+3.7	+5.1

Source: Based on data from Institute for Fiscal Studies (2010)

Given that poverty is a highly abstract concept, a perfect substitutability of various indicators would be surprising. But in the measurement of poverty, the sensitivity of the results to the choice of a measurement is extraordinary. Table 4 shows how figures for *income inequality* (as opposed to poverty) differ depending on how 'inequality' is measured. It shows the results obtained from five common definitions of inequality, applied to 28 OECD countries.[1] Different income inequality measures, too, produce diverging results, but correlations of 0.80 or above are common.[2] When evaluating inequality, the choice of the measure is not trivial, but it is unlikely to shape the entire outcome – this is quite unlike the situation when we try to measure poverty.

Table 4 **Correlation between standard measures of income inequality applied to 28 OECD countries**

	Gini-coefficient	Mean log deviation	Standard coefficient of variation	Interdecile ratio P90/ P10	Interdecile ratio P50/ P10
Gini- coefficient	1.00	0.99	0.80	0.97	0.88
Mean log deviation		1.00	0.82	0.97	0.89
Standard coefficient of variation			1.00	0.80	0.62
Interdecile ratio P90/P10				1.00	0.94
Interdecile ratio P50/P10					1.00

Source: Based on data from OECD (2008: 51)

This sensitivity of poverty measurement to the choice of indicator is seldom explicitly mentioned in public policy debates.

[1] The Netherlands and New Zealand were omitted because data was partially missing.

[2] The exception is the association between the coefficient of variation, which is most sensitive to inequalities at the top of the distribution, and the P50/P10 ratio, which ignores the upper half of the distribution completely.

Instead, policymakers as well as charities and NGOs concerned with the topic often seem to assume that different poverty indices are merely different approximations of the same underlying concept. The figures resulting from the application of the most common poverty concept are therefore frequently quoted as 'the number of people living below the poverty line' or 'the number of people living in poverty' (see, for example, Gregg et al., 1999; Child Poverty Action Group, 2000; Save the Children, 2000; Barnardo's, 2001).

Now that we have established the importance of the chosen measure of poverty, the next chapter will explore how the common understanding of poverty has itself changed over time in the developed world, and especially in the UK. While thus far the statistical properties of particular indices have been emphasised, the next chapter will place the emphasis on the poverty concept behind these measurements.

4 THE UNDERSTANDING OF POVERTY OVER TIME

Early poverty measures

Historically, understanding of poverty has been related to a concept of physical functioning. It was interpreted as a lack of resources necessary to fulfil 'essential' physical needs, such as nutrition, shelter and clothing. In Britain, systematic attempts to measure poverty go back to the late nineteenth century. Data documenting the living standards of the poorest had been gathered long before (Gordon, 2006: 37–9). But it is Charles Booth who is associated with the first use of explicit, monetary poverty lines: thresholds that separated the poor from the non-poor. This enabled him to compose his poverty maps of London, which categorised boroughs by their prevalence of poverty (Glennerster, 2004: 18–21; Fearon, n.d.). Booth never explained where his threshold, which he labelled the 'line of poverty', came from. Gillie (1996) observes a striking similarity to the London School Board's eligibility criteria for the reimbursement of tuition fees for poor parents, so Booth may have taken the poverty line from the school board's calculations. It was Benjamin Seebohm Rowntree who first became associated with the development of a systematic poverty indicator. Poverty, for him, was present when 'total earnings are insufficient to supply adequate food, clothing and shelter for the maintenance of merely physical health' (Rowntree, 1922: 54).

To translate this concept into an indicator, Rowntree assembled a consumption basket containing a specific quantity and quality of food, housing, clothing and several household-related items. The composition of the basket was determined by a combination of experts' judgements on what constituted 'minimum requirements', and on the spending patterns Rowntree observed. For the food element, Rowntree tried to assemble a list of essential nutrients that reflected a consensus among nutritional experts on a minimum healthy diet (ibid.: 88–103). The list was then transformed into a food basket gathering all these nutrients at a low cost (ibid.: 103–6). For the rent element, Rowntree recorded the rents actually paid, and assumed that since his investigations took place in poor neighbourhoods, typical rents in these areas already represented the necessary minimum (ibid.: 106). The poverty line was equal to the total cost of acquiring all elements in the basket. People were classified to be in 'primary poverty' if their income fell below the cost of the basket. Rowntree's 1899 measure was an extremely ascetic, pure subsistence standard:

> A family living upon the scale allowed for in this estimate must never spend a penny on railway fare or omnibus ... They must never purchase a halfpenny newspaper or spend a penny to buy a ticket for a popular concert. They must write no letters to absent children ... They cannot save, nor can they join a sick club or Trade Union ... The children must have no pocket money for dolls, marbles, or sweets. The father must smoke no tobacco, and must drink no beer. The mother must never buy any pretty clothes for herself or for her children ... Should a child fall ill, it must be attended by the parish doctor; should it die, it must be buried by the parish. (Ibid.: 134)

Other poverty studies carried out in the first half of the twentieth century followed the Budget Standard Approach and also used baskets of necessities (Horton and Gregory, 2009: 1–6; Pichaud and Webb, 2004: 33–47). This can therefore be considered the dominant poverty concept of that time.

It becomes apparent that for Rowntree and those operating within his framework poverty is an 'objective' phenomenon, ultimately manifesting itself in a person's physical constitution. In order to measure the type of poverty referred to here, little knowledge of the time and place which form the background of the investigation is required. There is hardly any reference to customary tastes and preferences, and general economic conditions are referred to only insofar as they affect the employment prospects of the interviewees.

Criticisms of Rowntree's work – and Rowntree's response

A puzzling feature of Rowntree's work was the high degree of what he labelled 'secondary poverty' – the situation of families who possessed enough resources to begin with, but spent them 'unwisely', and therefore did not have essentials. Misspending included 'ignorant extravagance, gambling, or expenditure upon drink' (Rowntree, 1922: 29–30). Given the restrictive nature of the indicator, some degree of spending 'inefficiency' would not have been surprising, and was in fact virtually inevitable. But those in 'secondary poverty' represented almost two-thirds of the whole poverty population (ibid.: 298), a highly unconvincing outcome. Why would a majority of those living in poverty deliberately and continuously deprive themselves of the necessities required for physical functioning?

Decades later, in the 1950s and 1960s, Peter Townsend and Brian Abel-Smith offered an alternative explanation for this apparent paradox. Townsend questioned the relevance of Booth/Rowntree-type poverty indicators because of the way they were detached from people's observed consumption patterns:

> How those on the borderline of poverty ought to spend
> their money is a very different thing from how they do
> spend their money. It would be unrealistic to expect them,
> as in effect many social investigators have expected them,
> to be skilled dieticians with marked tendencies towards
> Puritanism. (Townsend, 1954: 133)

Townsend's main criticism was not that the Booth/Rowntree poverty standards were overly restrictive, which could, perhaps, have been resolved by allowing for a higher margin of spending inefficiency. Townsend found that the Budget Standard Approach contained a systematic error. He observed that even when poor people experienced a severe lack of resources, they never devoted all of their spending to physical needs, but always reserved a share for activities related to social life and social conventions.

By focusing merely on physical needs and ignoring social ones, Rowntree-type measures ignored the fact that people do not live in a vacuum, but in a social context, and that this necessarily affected their spending behaviour. Participating in wider society, people could not autonomously dispose of their resources like Robinson Crusoe on a lonely island, because participation came at a cost: 'The pattern of spending among poor people is largely determined by the accepted modes of behaviour in the communities in which they live.'

This refers to expenses which could be labelled 'social participation costs' or 'social inclusion costs', and which can include a particular standard of clothing or attendance at social events. Inability to meet these expenses does not affect a person's health, and scarcely meets Rowntree's 'physical efficiency' criteria. But it can result in a state of social exclusion.

It could be argued that Townsend's criticism could still have been accommodated *within* the Booth/Rowntree framework, instead of requiring a fundamentally new definition of poverty. In devising the list of essentials, the focus could have been extended to include not only physical efficiency, but also social participation.

On the one hand, this would have required the inclusion of one or several additional components to the existing ones of food, housing, clothing and household goods. Social and/or cultural activities could have been included as a category in their own right, while the aspect of 'social inclusion' could have shaped the selection of items for the other categories. This would have meant that in the clothing category, items would be selected not only by their appropriateness to protect from weather, but also by their suitability for appearing in public, given time-specific and place-specific conventions.

In fact, in his second and third poverty studies (from 1936 and 1950), Rowntree did go a few steps in this direction. The 1936 study amended the old poverty measure by an additional category labelled 'personal sundries', containing items which are not essential for physical survival but enable participation in social life. It included a daily newspaper, stamps, writing paper and books.

Social participation considerations also entered the selection of items in other categories. For the clothing category, he included 'just what is necessary to keep the body warm and dry *and to maintain a moderate respectability*' (Linsley and Linsley, 1993: 94, emphasis added). For the food category, he selected a diet that was 'as economic as possible, *having regard for national customs*' (ibid., emphasis added).

On balance, though, Rowntree remained faithful to his original framework, in which poverty was impeded physical functioning, not impeded social participation. The 'personal sundries' category is arguably misnamed, because about half of the expenditure in that category was related to predominantly physical needs, not social needs. For example, Rowntree seemed to interpret membership in Friendly Society sick clubs as a social activity, and not, as seems much more appropriate, as health insurance costs. In the clothing category, 'there is nothing allowed for mere show' (ibid.), and he conceded that it was unlikely that many people actually chose a diet close to the one he had selected.

These amendments may have made Rowntree's poverty studies more socially relevant. But mixing a notion of social participation into Rowntree's original physical sustenance indicator was like mixing oil into water. Rowntree himself noted that it was difficult to reconcile the new elements with his overarching goal of objectivity: 'In the matter of expenditure upon personal sundries, I was forced to rely largely upon my own judgement, since it is far less easy to fix a standard for such items as beer and tobacco, amusements and holidays, than it is for clothing and fuel' (ibid.: 95).

In short, Rowntree made limited attempts to incorporate social needs into his physical needs concept, but they remained alien elements in his basket. Unlike for physical needs, Rowntree had no criterion for recognising and selecting social needs. This is the structural break between Rowntree's and Townsend's understandings of poverty.

For Townsend, there were no purely physical needs. Needs were an almost entirely social concept. They were linked to the development of overall living standards: 'Poverty is not an absolute state. It is relative deprivation. Society itself is continuously changing and thrusting new obligations on its members. They, in turn, develop new needs. They are rich or poor according to their share of the resources that are available to all' (Townsend, 1962: 225).

The discovery of 'relative poverty'

In British academia, Townsend's research gained ground in the 1960s, probably amplified by the ascent of Runciman's (1966) related but not identical concept of 'relative deprivation'. Runciman showed that individuals and groups did not evaluate their material living standards in a vacuum, but relative to benchmark standards, usually those of other groups in society. His theory was meant to explain why social unrest sometimes arose in times when absolute living standards were actually rising.

Though they are sometimes used as synonyms, 'relative deprivation' is not the same as relative poverty. The former is not about income gaps per se, but about income gaps that are perceived as unmerited and alterable by the members of the less well-off groups. Hence, inequality need not be especially high for relative deprivation to occur, when a small lead by the better-off is perceived to be unmerited. On the other hand, relative deprivation need not occur when inequalities are large but widely tolerated by the less well-off.

Relative poverty, in contrast, is purely a function of the income distribution, regardless of how it arises and how it is being perceived. But both concepts coincide in directing the focus of attention away from people's absolute command over material resources, and towards distributional considerations.

In the US context, Galbraith (1958) endorsed a relativist notion of poverty in his work *The Affluent Society*:

> People are poverty-stricken when their income, even if adequate for survival, falls markedly behind that of the community. Then they cannot have what the larger community regards as the minimum necessary for decency; and they cannot wholly escape, therefore, the judgment of the larger community that they are indecent. (Ibid.: 323–4)

The research of Fuchs (1965) in the USA took the same line: 'Attempts to define poverty in absolute terms are doomed to failure because they run contrary to man's nature as a social animal.'

This change in perspective contributed to what would later be labelled the 'rediscovery of poverty' in the 1960s (Pichaud and Webb, 2004: 45–7). It represented a radical break with the optimistic outlook of the immediate post-war era, which assumed that with general economic progress, supported by a limited safety net, societies would eventually outgrow poverty. This notion of 'growing out of poverty' was linked to a poverty concept of impeded physical functioning in the Booth/Rowntree sense, a measure which had fallen so drastically by the 1950s.

When poverty is, instead, interpreted as impeded social participation, and needs as inherently relative, then economic progress ceases to be a force that can by itself lift people out of poverty. Poverty is no longer viewed as a lack of material resources per se. It is a lack of material resources *insofar* as these are necessary to comply with contemporary social norms.

These norms, it was argued, inevitably became more demanding as societies grew wealthier. Participation in mainstream society thus becomes costlier with rising average living standards and the effect of economic progress on poverty becomes an ambiguous one. On the one hand, across-the-board growth raises the material living standards of the poor. But, at the same time, it raises social norms and expectations, and thus the cost of social inclusion which the poor face. Gains experienced by the middle classes now become a liability for the poor according to this argument. It results in 'new obligations and expectations placed on members of the community' (Townsend, 1979: 53), or more explicitly, 'as a society's standard of living rises, more expensive consumption is forced on the poor to remain integrated into society' (Brady, 2003a: 9).

This new understanding of poverty gradually replaced the old one. By the early 1980s, Sen (1983) had already noted an 'emerging unanimity in favour of taking a relative as opposed to an absolutist view of poverty' (ibid.: 167). The near-unanimity he mentions really did emerge, and remains present to this day. Scruggs and Allan (2006) note that 'research has focused almost exclusively on relative poverty rates ... Virtually all studies of the determinants of national poverty and most comparative descriptions of poverty rates in the LIS[1] countries use the concept of relative poverty' (pp. 881–3).

This shift has not been universally welcomed. A common objection has been that relative indicators are completely detached from the command of the poor over goods and services. The low-income strata in a wealthy but unequal society

---

1 The LIS countries are those which participate in the Luxembourg Income Studies.

could be materially better off than their counterparts in a poor but egalitarian society (e.g. Sarlo, 2007; Clark et al., 2006; Lomasky and Swan, 2009). Keeping the rationale behind relative measures, as outlined above, in mind, this line of criticism would miss the point. Relative poverty is not meant to be a measure of command over goods and services. It is meant to be a measure of social inclusion. Defenders of the relativist concept would argue that in the poor egalitarian society, the low-income strata may consume fewer goods and services but that they are able to participate in most activities considered 'customary' in their society, which may not be the case in the wealthy and unequal society.

Sen (1983) noted that relative indicators can display low poverty amid starvation, as long as poverty extends sufficiently far up the income distribution. Most advocates of relative standards, however, do not argue that this measure is applicable to developing countries. The most common position is that absolute poverty is the appropriate focus for developing countries, while developed countries should concentrate on the more 'ambitious' relative measure (Brady, 2003a: 8; New Policy Institute & Joseph Rowntree Foundation, n.d.; European Commission, 2004). Ravallion and Chen's (2009) measure, which is relative, but equipped with an absolute lower bound for the poverty line, formalises this idea.

According to adherents of the relative notion, there is no such thing as 'absolute poverty', but only different kinds of relativity. UNICEF Innocenti Research Center (2005) calls the distinction a 'false polarization': 'A workable definition of poverty will ... always be related to time and place ... All practicable definitions of poverty are ultimately definitions of relative poverty' (ibid.: 6–7).

'Related to time and place' ultimately means 'related to overall economic development'. There may be huge, legitimate disagreements over what precisely constitutes poverty in the context of a present-day Britain. But there is virtual unanimity that electricity, heating, hot running water and an indoor bathroom constitute minimum necessities (see Gordon et al., 2000; and Patanzis et al., 2006). Yet there is nothing 'natural' or 'obvious' about our present understanding of poverty. The above-mentioned items would not have been considered necessities by a majority in, say, the 1930s. A poverty standard incorporating the mentioned items could not be meaningfully applied retrospectively to the year 1930. It would produce an extremely high poverty rate including many people who, at that time, would not have been considered poor by anybody. Such an approach would only be defensible when assuming that poverty is somehow 'objective', and that people lacking these items in 1930 *were* poor even if they did not know they were poor. Similarly, a poverty standard of some distant future will produce extremely high poverty rates when applied retrospectively to the year 2010. In 2090, amenities which are as yet unheard of will be considered 'necessities' with the same near-unanimity with which we consider electricity and indoor bathrooms necessities today (see Karelis, 2007, on these considerations).

A poverty standard that can be meaningfully applied to the year 2010 must differ sharply from a poverty standard that can be meaningfully applied to the year 1930, and both must differ sharply from one that will be meaningful in 2090. As long as living standards rise over time, poverty standards need to be upgraded over time to remain socially relevant, adjusting in some way to changes in economic circumstances and social perceptions. This observation alone, however, does not justify the use of relative poverty for measurement of government policy purposes, as we shall see later.

As the relative position gained acceptance, the change in the accepted view of poverty eventually translated into a change in the measurement of poverty. In Britain as well as in other developed nations, it became common to set the poverty line as a fixed fraction of mean or median incomes. It should be noted that Townsend himself was rather critical of these particular specifications of the relative poverty concept for involving an arbitrary cut-off point (Gordon, 2006: 32–3).

In 1981, the European Commission (1981) adopted a definition of poverty as referring to 'individuals or families whose resources are so small as to exclude them from a minimum acceptable way of life in the Member State in which they live' (ibid.). Reports measuring poverty on an EU-wide scale followed, setting poverty lines at 50 per cent of each member state's mean income (Atkinson, 1998: 2–3). Since the beginning of the 2000s, the European Union and UNICEF have regularly compiled internationally harmonised relative poverty indicators (Eurostat, 2005; UNICEF Innocenti Research Center, 2005, 2007). The concept is also used by the OECD, the World Bank and the International Monetary Fund, even though these organisations do not express a corporate view about relative poverty (see OECD, 2008; Ravallion and Chen, 2009; Nielsen, 2009).

In the UK, the Department of Social Security began publishing figures of relative income poverty in the 1980s (Hills, 2004: 40), even though the UK government at this time strongly disapproved of the concept (see House of Commons, 1990). In the late 1990s, the New Labour government explicitly embraced the relative poverty concept by making it the basis of official policy targets.

Most notably, this involved quantitative targets for the reduction and eventual eradication of relative child poverty. A similar pledge to eradicate relative pensioner poverty followed (Stewart et al., 2009: 10–12), though no numerical targets were specified for this latter aim.

Soon after, the relative view of poverty ceased to be a dividing line between the political camps, with the Conservative Party and the Liberal Democrats committing themselves to the same concept (Hunt and Clark, 2007; Liberal Democrats, 2007; Conservative Party, 2008). Most explicitly, David Cameron remarked:

> In the past we used to think of poverty in absolute terms ... That's not enough. We need to think of poverty in relative terms – the fact that some people lack those things which others in society take for granted. So I want this message to go out loud and clear – the Conservative Party recognises, will measure and will act on relative poverty. (BBC News, 2006).

In short, relative poverty has become, as Hills (2004: 42) put it, 'the nearest that the UK has to an official poverty line'.

5 THE 'REDISCOVERY OF POVERTY' IN THE 1960S AND THE REBOUND OF POVERTY IN THE 1980S

As described, local surveys carried out during the first half of the twentieth century suggest that poverty, despite severe temporary setbacks, was characterised by a long-term downward trend. If there had been no change in the common understanding of the concept, then the mainstream interpretation today would be that poverty as a social phenomenon disappeared in the post-war decades. Yet the emerging interpretation of poverty as a relative concept conveyed a completely different impression. Relative rates were always substantially higher than even an amended Rowntree indicator could have been, but, more importantly, they showed no downward trend at all. They showed a stubborn inertia amid rising real incomes towards the bottom of the distribution. Relative poverty was largely flat throughout the 1960s, 1970s and early 1980s. The year 1984 then became the starting point of a sharp rebound in relative poverty. For the rest of the decade, poverty rose in every year, and finally settled at a new longer-term average at a much higher level. It was only from the late 1990s that a new downward trend set in, but it never came near to reversing the previous rebound.

This evolution of relative poverty rates has given rise to a particular 'poverty narrative', in the sense of a widely accepted interpretation of the evolution of poverty in post-war history. Patanzis et al. (2006) provide the following account:

During the 1960s, just over 10% of the population lived in a low-income household. This rose slightly under the Conservative administration and following the oil shock in the 1970s, and then declined to about 8% during the mid-1970s. In 1979 ... changes in economic and social policy resulted in a trebling of the proportion of people living in low-income households from 8% to 25% – clearly showing that governments do have an effect on the amount of poverty in a country and that social policy does make a difference. (Ibid.: 4)

For Horton and Gregory (2009: 4–10), poverty in post-war Britain has emerged in a U-shaped manner, defined by two decisive turning points. They see the foundation of the post-war welfare state as the onset of a sustained decline in poverty. The policies of the 1980s, which the authors view as an era of 'welfare retrenchment', represent the second turning point (the bottom of the 'U'). In their account, the subsequent 'huge increase in poverty' represents 'one of the greatest social transformations of modern times'. Stewart et al. (2009: 2) also believe that poverty has rebounded since the 1980s, eventually reaching levels 'unprecedented in post-war history'. This interpretation has become widespread among researchers, policymakers, non-governmental organisations and charities (see Andrews and Jacobs, 1990; Glynn and Booth, 1996; Jones and Novak, 1999; Kastendiek, 1999; Kelly, 1999; Gregg et al., 1999; Child Poverty Action Group, 2000; Save the Children, 2000; Barnardo's, 2001; Sefton et al., 2009; Stewart et al., 2009).

In this sense, the 'rediscovery of poverty' in the 1960s was the precondition for the 'rebound of poverty' in the 1980s. This interpretation could not have emerged within a Rowntreean poverty

Figure 6   **Relative versus (quasi-) absolute poverty in the UK 1961–2008, both after housing costs (AHC)**

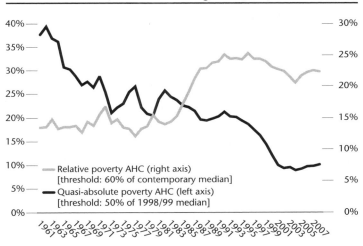

Source: Based on data from Institute for Fiscal Studies (2010). The measures are plotted on different axes because their levels are not meaningfully comparable

framework, or in any other framework which does not tie the poverty line tightly to average incomes. Figure 6 shows the evolution of relative poverty after housing costs (AHC) against a quasi-absolute measure of poverty AHC in which the poverty line is set at 50 per cent of the real median income for 1998/99. While not tending towards zero (for reasons that will be explored later), the absolute measure shows a long-term downward trend.

The change in the common understanding of poverty has coined a particular narrative of post-war history, and of the social and economic policies that shaped it, which might otherwise not have arisen.

6 DIFFERENT MEASURES, DIFFERENT POLICIES

It was shown above that different poverty definitions provide different results and conclusions. These are not random differences, but systematically different impressions about the drivers of changes in poverty. They lead to vastly different policy conclusions. This is especially true when comparing the two most well-known concepts, relative poverty and absolute poverty.

A number of poverty studies have used regression models treating the poverty rate as the dependent variable, and decomposing it into its explanatory factors. Unsurprisingly, the variables which are identified as the main drivers of poverty rates depend to a large degree on whether poverty is measured in an absolute or in a relative sense. The purchasing power of those at the bottom of a distribution, and the distance between the bottom and the middle of the distribution, are shaped by different factors.

Harberger (1998) focuses on absolute living standards of those at the bottom of the income distribution in a number of countries at various stages of economic development: most of these countries are transition economies. He argues: 'nothing in our experience suggests that the real level of welfare of, say, the bottom quintile of a society does not improve as economic growth takes place' (ibid.: 203).

In his framework, policy recommendations to fight poverty largely coincide with policy recommendations to promote overall economic growth. He recommends a few targeted interventions directed towards poor people, such as support for access to healthcare and education facilities. But, apart from this, his recommendations for addressing poverty are virtually identical to general 'good governance': monetary stability, free trade and accountable public institutions.

Looking at a sample of 92 countries over the second half of the twentieth century, Dollar and Kraay (2001) find further empirical evidence for this notion. They regress average incomes of people in the bottom quintile against GDP per capita and a set of other variables, to find that growth benefits the poor about as much as other income strata, and perhaps more.[1] The authors' conclusion is straightforward: 'growth is good for the poor'.

The anti-poverty policies they recommend include strengthening the rule of law, providing a stable currency, limiting government spending, permitting free trade and enabling the development of sophisticated capital markets. Again, these are also major factors that boost economic development in general. In the framework of Dollar and Kraay, and of Harberger, there is hardly any difference between poverty alleviation and boosting overall economic performance.

But most analyses which model poverty rates as a function of economic, policy-related and socio-demographic variables are based on relative indicators. Contrary to the above findings, they usually conclude that economic growth is of minor importance or even irrelevant for lowering poverty. Growth-promoting policies are therefore not considered poverty-reducing. It is redistributive efforts which become the most important determinant of poverty.

---

1   The elasticity of the income of the poor with regard to average income is 1.19, but the authors cannot verify that the difference from 1 is statistically significant.

Scruggs and Allan (2006) specify a model in which a country's poverty rate depends on the generosity of the welfare benefits it provides,[2] growth rates, and a number of additional variables. The authors find that 'generous welfare benefits play some nontrivial role in reducing poverty' (ibid.: 901) while 'growth rates are not statistically significant' (ibid.: 900–901). Kenworthy (1998) specifies a similar model and reaches similar conclusions.[3]

Brady (2003b) takes this approach a step farther and uses a model in which a country's poverty rate is explained not just by economic conditions and social policy, but also by the political power balance. He finds that 'none of the economic and demographic variables consistently affect state-mediated poverty'[4] (ibid.: 571). Instead, 'left political institutions trigger an expansion of the welfare state. As past research also demonstrates, this welfare-state expansion reduces state-mediated poverty' (ibid.: 577).

An even more comprehensive model of this type has been specified by Moller et al. (2003). They agree with Brady that 'when states spend more of their financial resources on citizen welfare, poverty is reduced. When they spend it under the influence of left-wing parties, they spend it in a more redistributive way and

2   Welfare generosity is measured as an index summarising key features of welfare programmes such as replacement rates, the restrictiveness of eligibility criteria, coverage, and the existence of time limits.

3   Both Scruggs and Allan and Kenworthy also repeat their analysis using absolute, instead of RP, as a dependent variable, and conclude that welfare spending also reduces AP. In both models, however, pre-tax/pre-transfer poverty is included as an independent variable. Specifying the model in this way almost certainly produces this outcome. Neither Scruggs and Allan nor Kenworthy examine the effect of growth on pre-transfer poverty itself.

4   'State-mediated poverty' is the poverty rate obtained when looking at incomes after taxes and transfers.

are particularly effective at reducing poverty' (ibid.: 44). In their model, economic development contributes to poverty reduction only up to a certain point, beyond which it does the opposite. This 'U-turn', the authors hypothesise, is defined by the transitions from an industry-centred to a service-centred economy, and from a national to a globally integrated economy. Globalisation and structural change are drivers of poverty.

While not explicitly rejecting growth or endorsing a particular political ideology, a host of other authors have also shown that, controlled for other factors, the size of the welfare budget (or a similar variable) is the major factor in reducing poverty (Mitchel, 1991; Förster, 1993; Korpi and Palme, 1998; Kim, 2000; Lohmann, 2006; Marx, 2007).

These findings from academia are mirrored by the recommendations provided by government institutions and the NGO community. Eurostat (2005) looks at the effect of social transfer spending on relative poverty and finds that 'social transfers ... have an important redistributive effect that helps reduce the number of people who are at risk of poverty ... In the absence of all social transfers, the poverty risk for the EU population as a whole would be considerably higher than it is in reality (40% instead of 16%)' (ibid.: 4).

In the UK, the policy demands of the poverty advocacy community are centred on distributional issues. The Child Poverty Action Group (2009) makes the case for higher top-income tax rates, higher inheritance taxes and a more progressive structure of council tax (pp. 44–6), combined with higher out-of-work benefits and in-work benefits (pp. 24–5). These demands follow directly from how the organisation views poverty: 'Poverty can only be understood in relation to social norms, and sustainable reductions are only possible if policies address the wider income inequality that drives it' (p. 18).

In the absolute-poverty-centred framework, poverty reduction largely coincides with economic policies boosting overall economic progress. In the relative-poverty-centred framework, poverty reduction is at best viewed as a separate set of policies that barely overlap with general economic policies. The focus is on redistributive social policies.

This enthusiasm for social spending is somewhat surprising because even within the relativist framework, the case for heavily redistributive policies does not automatically emerge. Higher social spending does not automatically lead to a more equal income distribution. It has been intensively documented that the political process is often driven by the interests of well-organised, politically influential groups (see Tullock, 1976) rather than compassion for the least fortunate. In the political sphere (in our role as voters, members of citizens' initiatives, pressure groups, etc.), most of us act no more altruistically than in our role as market participants. Far from representing a kind of institutionalised altruism, welfare states are subject to the same favour-seeking behaviour as other policy areas (see, e.g., Goodin and Le Grand, 1987).

The impression of an inverse relationship between income inequality and the size of the welfare state largely arises because social policy debates are often centred on the distinction between an 'Anglo-Saxon model' and a 'Nordic model', for which this relationship holds broadly. The Mediterranean countries, however, are characterised by large income disparities *and* large social spending budgets. The opposite is observable in Switzerland, where inequality of market incomes (income before taxes and transfers) is moderate to begin with. If the Swiss government did not engage in any redistribution at all, Switzerland would reach the same Gini-coefficient[5] of income inequality as Italy does *with* its present level of government redistribution.

Table 5 **Social spending versus income inequality**

	High social spending (public cash transfers > 15% of working-age households' disposable income)	Low social spending (public cash transfers < 10% of working-age households' disposable income)
Low inequality (Gini-coefficient < 0.28)	Sweden Denmark	Switzerland
High inequality (Gini-coefficient > 0.32)	Greece Italy Portugal	USA

Source: Statistics gleaned from OECD (2008)

In a number of countries, including Greece, Italy and Portugal, middle-class households receive larger sums in transfer payments than low-income households. When transfers are regressive, redistribution to poorer households occurs only indirectly, through middle-class households contributing much more in taxes and social security contributions than poor households. In a somewhat separate but related argument it could also be pointed out that there is evidence that benefits in kind provided by the government, such as education, are of much higher quality for the better off because of their ability to articulate concerns and desires through the political system.

5   The Gini-coefficient is a standard measure of income inequality. It plots a country's income distribution against a hypothetical distribution of perfect equality and measures the deviation. A value of 0 would correspond to a society where all incomes are equal; a value of 1 to a society where one individual possesses everything and the rest nothing.

On average, developed countries with a higher level of welfare spending do achieve a more egalitarian income distribution – though this is not necessarily the case. This is why the above-mentioned social models find a negative relationship between social spending and relative poverty. There is, though, not the same relationship between the material hardship of the poor and the level of social spending.

7 GROWTH VERSUS REDISTRIBUTION

The aim of compressing the income distribution collides with the aim of across-the-board income growth. Growth-inhibiting effects of redistribution arise at two levels. First, redistributive policies necessarily involve the taxation of income, savings, wealth, consumption, or a mixture thereof, thus discouraging productive economic activities. Second, redistribution involves the payment of transfers based on particular conditions such as unemployment. They thereby reduce incentives to prevent these conditions from arising, to make individual provisions in case they arise nonetheless, and to overcome them quickly once they have arisen.

Implications for taxation

On the first point, there is ample empirical evidence that both higher levels of taxation and a steeper tax progression are harmful to economic development. Heath (2006) provides a summary of the empirical literature of models regressing growth rates or GDP levels against a set of potential explanatory variables, including taxes. With huge differences in emphasis and magnitude, much, though not all, of the evidence points towards growth-impeding effects of taxes on earned income, capital gains or business profits (ibid.: 28–37).

The cross-country evidence is not fully conclusive, which is hardly surprising since tax systems, and indeed whole economies, differ in a multitude of aspects which are hard to quantify. Empirical models account for cross-country differences only in crude ways.[1] There are cross-country studies which fail to find a significant impact of taxation on growth and, in particular, the economic success of the Scandinavian countries is often presented as 'proof' that even very high levels of taxation were not harmful provided the money was well spent.

Evidence from within-country time series, however, is more conclusive. A notable example is the recent estimate of several countries' 'Laffer curves' provided by Trabandt and Uhlig (2009). They find that Sweden and Denmark have almost reached the peak of their respective Laffer curves for the taxation of labour, while for the taxation of capital, they are already beyond the tax-revenue-maximising level (ibid.: 20–26). If the Scandinavian governments decreased taxes on labour such as income tax, the work-encouraging effects would be so large that the initial loss of tax revenue would be almost fully offset, according to this model. Decreasing taxes on capital would even lead to a net rise in tax revenue through encouraging greater capital formation. Taxation discourages productive activities and shrinks the tax base, with Scandinavia being neither an exception nor a proof of the contrary.

The size of the shadow economy also provides a rough idea of whether tax levels are 'too high' for a given cultural setting. Schneider (2006) provides a summary of the empirical evidence

---

1   For example, a model that contains the average tax rate and the top marginal tax rate reveals little about how the tax code treats deductions, write-offs, capital depreciation, fiscal drag, allowances, etc.

on the determinants of the size of the shadow economy, and finds: 'In almost all studies it has been found out, that the tax and social security contribution burdens are one of the main causes for the existence of the shadow economy.'

The relationship between the size of the state and the shadow economy is, of course, not a mechanistic one. Unobservable cultural factors apparently play a role, with Scandinavians showing a high tolerance towards taxation. But a hidden economy amounting to 17–19 per cent of GDP demonstrates that even Scandinavians are not willing or able to shoulder a tax burden of any size. Nowhere in Europe, except Switzerland, does the hidden economy account for less than 10 per cent of GDP, and even in economies commonly associated with 'small government' and 'light taxes', sizeable proportions of economic activities are driven into illicitness. Given that the informal sector, operating outside the legal framework, is less productive than the formal one, and that evasion itself comes at a cost, these figures point to a substantial economic cost of taxation.

So if the Scandinavian economies perform well nevertheless, it is because they manage to compensate for their high levels of taxation in other ways, not because these high levels are not harmful. In the rankings of economic freedom, Sweden and Denmark rank exceptionally well in all economic policy areas except fiscal freedom and government spending (see Fraser Institute, 2009; Heritage Foundation, 2010).[2] This can be shown by excluding these two categories from the index, and recalculating

---

2   'Fiscal freedom' is a summary measure of top marginal tax rates on individual and corporate income, and of the total taxation ratio. 'Government spending' is simply a function that decreases in total government expenditure. For a given level of government spending, the Fiscal Freedom score can vary depending on how 'flat' the structure of taxation is.

the summary score with the remaining eight.[3] On this 'rump index', shown in the second to last column of Table 6, Denmark achieves the highest score in the world.

Table 6 **Summary measures of fiscal exploitation and counterbalances**

	Degree to which a cut in labour taxes would refinance itself	Degree to which a cut in capital taxes would refinance itself	Size of the shadow economy	Economic freedom score (0–100) when excluding fiscal freedom and government spending	Employment Commitment Index (1–5) men/women
Denmark	83%	137%	17.3%	90.2	3.82/3.90
Sweden	83%	109%	18.3%	83.8	3.53/3.77
EU-14	54%	79%	18.0%	–	
UK	42%	73%	12.2%	82.6	3.18/3.37
Ireland	35%	50%	15.3%	85.0	3.47/3.51
USA	32%	51%	8.7%	81.8	3.48/3.48

Sources: Statistics from Trabandt and Uhlig (2009); Schneider (2006); Heritage Foundation (2010); Esser (2009)

Specifically for the UK, the Institute for Fiscal Studies provides estimates on the responsiveness of top incomes, which are especially important for redistributive aims, to top-income tax rates. This can be interpreted as a quasi-Laffer curve for the taxation of the highest incomes. Based on time-series data, they find a very strong responsiveness. Decreasing the net-of-tax rate (100 per cent minus the marginal tax rate) by 1 per cent would decrease

3   The remaining categories are: business freedom, trade freedom, monetary freedom, investment freedom, financial freedom, property rights, freedom from corruption, and labour freedom.

taxable top incomes by 0.46 per cent. According to this estimate, the taxation of top earners is already in the revenue-maximising region, so that a further intensification of fiscal exploitation would not raise additional tax revenue (Browne, 2010; Brewer and Browne, 2006). These estimates do not include the economic impact of a reduction in top earners' work effort.

Based on a model considering the overall tax burden, Smith (2006: 77–84) estimates the long-term cost associated with taxation in terms of depressed growth rates. He finds that, if the share of government spending in the UK had remained constant since 1960, national output in 2005 would have been at least twice as high as it actually was. Smith does not cover the distributional impact which a freeze of the relative size of government would have had. But if the growth–redistribution trade-off is of a magnitude anywhere near Smith's estimate, it is extremely unlikely that the poor would not be better off in absolute terms today had the low-tax/high-growth strategy been pursued.

Perverse results from the relativist framework

There is also ample empirical evidence that high welfare payments discourage people from taking up work and/or progressing in the labour market. A summary of the empirical literature by Krueger and Meyer (2002) shows that, controlled for other factors, higher out-of-work benefits are largely associated with a lower search effort, higher reservation wages and ultimately longer unemployment spells. Longer unemployment spells, in turn, have been shown to be associated with a depreciation of human capital (Pissarides, 1992) and thus a reduction of future employment prospects.

An alternative interpretation holds that an extensive safety net *increases* people's willingness to get involved with the vicissitudes of the modern labour market. Horton and Gregory (2009: 87) argue that 'people's employment commitment tends to be stronger in countries with more generous benefits than in those with less generous benefits'. But this interpretation has its pitfalls. What the authors mean by 'employment commitment' is an index formed from an international attitudes survey, where people are asked to what extent they agree with the following statements:

1. 'I would enjoy having a paid job even if I did not need the money.'
2. 'A job is just a way of earning money – no more.'

Measured in this way, employment commitment is indeed strongest in Scandinavia and weakest in the English-speaking countries (Esser, 2009). But this is not a proof that high welfare benefits 'create' a strong work ethic. What this index really measures (assuming that people's 'stated preferences' coincide broadly with their 'revealed preferences') is the extent to which people derive benefits from employment over and above the financial ones. Therefore, it is at least equally plausible to interpret the figures in a different way. It could be argued that 'employment commitment' is a cultural variable exogenous to the welfare state. When employment commitment is high, people's labour market decisions will be less responsive to pecuniary incentives. If two otherwise identical countries differ only in employment commitment, then the labour market disincentive effects arising from a given level of welfare provision will be weaker in the country where employment commitment is stronger. The latter country can therefore 'afford' a larger welfare state.

Looking at political cultures more broadly, Saunders (2001: 30) also argues that 'social democratic welfare regimes based on generous entitlements ... are probably only sustainable in countries with relatively strong collectivistic cultures'.

The same considerations apply to other policy tools available to intervene in the distribution of market incomes. Historically, subsidies to declining industries, protective tariffs or limits on immigration have played a greater role than redistribution through the tax and benefit system, and such measures are fully compatible with some of the poverty studies quoted above. But, like redistributive measures, they hamper overall economic development and ultimately absolute living standards.

It is not necessarily the case that adherents of a relative view of poverty are unaware of this trade-off or deny its implications. But, within a relativist framework, the above arguments must be seen as beside the point. Poverty, in this framework, is not about a lack of material resources: it is about social exclusion. Further real income growth at the bottom will not reduce poverty as long as median incomes rise too.

Taking a closer look at what 'real income growth at the bottom' really means, in more tangible terms, raises doubts about this view. Table 7 shows an excerpt from the annual expenditure profile of an average household in 1957, the year when Harold Macmillan famously remarked that 'most of our people have never had it so good'. This is contrasted with an excerpt from the annual expenditure profile of the poorest income decile[4] in

---

4   Bottom decile when deciles are ordered by gross equivalised income.

2008 amid a severe recession. The poorest in 2008 had to reserve much smaller shares of their budgets for necessities such as food and clothing (which were, presumably, of a much higher quality and variety than was on offer in 1957). Consequently, in 2008, the poor had sizeable shares left for items commonly associated with quality-of-life aspects: the poor were better off in a recession in 2008 than the average household in the year in which they had 'never had it so good'. Yet within the relativist framework, it would appear that these improvements have contributed nothing to the betterment of the poor because their effects have been entirely 'eaten up' by the growth in median incomes.

Table 7 **Share of household budget dedicated to selected items: average households in 1957 versus poorest households in 2008**

	Average households in 1957	Poorest decile (by gross equivalised income) in 2008
Food	33%	17%
Clothing and footwear	10%	5%
Recreation and culture	n.a.	11%
Restaurants and hotels	n.a.	7%
Communication	n.a.	4%

Source: Based on data from the Office for National Statistics (2010a, 2008)

Table 8 shows lack of access to selected consumer goods for three countries with roughly the same rates of relative poverty. It provides a glimpse of how the daily life of the least well off differs across societies.[5]

---

5   As explained earlier, not all people lacking these items are also in relative poverty and vice versa.

Table 8 **Share of the population involuntarily lacking selected consumer goods (material deprivation)**

	UK	Estonia	Poland
TV	0.1%	0.5%	1.0%
Telephone	0.2%	1.6%	2.9%
Washing machine	0.5%	3.3%	1.2%
A meal with meat, chicken or fish every second day	4.5%	8.2%	28.4%
Car	4.9%	20.8%	22.6%
Indoor bath or shower*	0.0%	20.0%	9.0%
Indoor toilet for sole use*	1.0%	17.0%	7.0%

Sources: Eurostat (2009a); *Eurostat (2005b)

Within the relativist framework, the British poor appear no better off than the Estonian and the Polish poor, even though they possess so many amenities that the latter do not possess. Growth is a 'problem' in the relative poverty framework.

PART II: TOWARDS A NEW MEASURE OF POVERTY

'Everything that can be invented has been invented.'
Charles H. Duell, US Patent Office commissioner
(1899; attributed)

'Car engineering has been finalised. What else could follow?'

Karl Benz (1920)

'We are at a turning point in human history. For centuries the best way of improving the quality of life has been to raise material living standards. But we have now come to the end of what economic growth can do for developed countries.'

Richard Wilkinson and Kate Pickett (2009)

8 THE FLAWS OF RELATIVE MEASURES

'Relative to where?' The geographical question

With economic progress, social norms change, and so do perceptions of what is required to lead a 'decent' life. If we understand relativity in the sense of context dependency, the notion is uncontroversial. Over the past century, electricity, indoor bathrooms, telephones and a number of other items have passed from desirable amenities to necessities in the perception of most citizens, and this process will continue in the future. It is also true that consumption decisions are partially shaped by the 'compliance costs' of participating in wider society. Being unable to dress in a publicly presentable way, to buy a present when invited to a birthday party, or to attend social events with friends and acquaintances – these are manifestations of poverty, even if they do not involve hunger, cold or disease. As Townsend has shown, people with very scarce means are often willing to forgo essentials in order to meet the cost of social inclusion. The latter is related to overall levels of economic development and, in growing economies, it rises over time. Since Rowntree-style measures failed to take this social, dynamic dimension of poverty into account, it is for a good reason that they were abandoned.

Relative standards emerged as an alternative because they appeared to be rooted in their social context, and able to adapt to changes therein. But this would presuppose that the cost of social inclusion and attainment of a decent minimum standard grows linearly with average income. Adherents of relative standards have never explained why this should be the case.

In principle, information about how perceptions about the adequacy of living standards are affected by the observed living standards of others can be obtained from research on 'subjective wellbeing'. Such studies regress people's self-reported life satisfaction (or sometimes a narrower subset such as 'job satisfaction' or 'consumption satisfaction') against a set of variables deemed to affect wellbeing, such as age, family status, employment status, state of health, etc. These explanatory variables usually include both the respondent's income and the income of an imputed reference group (or the ratio of the two). The peer group's income usually enters negatively and significantly and it often seems to contribute about as much to a respondent's wellbeing as his or her own income. There is also evidence that comparison takes place 'upwards' rather than 'downwards': avoiding falling behind others seems to be a greater concern than getting ahead of others.

At first sight, this appears consistent with a relative interpretation of poverty. As the peer group's income rises, so does the cost of remaining integrated, which adversely affects those unable to keep up. These studies, however, find it difficult to identify who precisely constitutes this 'reference group'. A few social wellbeing studies assume that the reference group simply consists of the inhabitants of the national territory. They therefore include the national average income, or a similar variable, among the factors that are deemed to affect wellbeing (see Easterlin, 1995; Blanchflower and Oswald, 2004). Conventional relative poverty measures do the same thing: when poverty lines are tagged to the national median, the national territory is implicitly assumed to be the domain over which customary consumption habits are formed. But many authors assume a much narrower, localised reference group, defined at the level of the region (Ferrer-i-Carbonell, 2005; Blanchflower and Oswald, 2004, referring to the USA), the municipality (Luttmer, 2004; Clark and Oswald, 1996), or even the vicinity (Kuhn et al., 2008). All of these specifications show some explanatory power, suggesting that there is nothing special about the national level or the national median, as far as the formation of norms and expectations is concerned.

Poverty standards, too, could then be defined over territories different from the national one. Data on regional relative poverty rates, with the poverty line of each region tagged to the median income of that region itself (and not to the national median), have already been calculated (see Rainwater et al., 2003; Kangas and Ritakallio, 2004). The second column of Table 9 shows poverty rates in prosperous and less prosperous regions within selected countries. The third column shows the poverty rate that these regions would record if they seceded from their respective countries and became sovereign nations. Relative poverty rates would increase drastically in the more prosperous regions and fall substantially in the structurally weaker ones.

Regional standards are perfectly feasible within the premises of a relative understanding of poverty. Some customary leisure habits and social events are specific to regions – or, indeed, smaller localities – rather than to nation-states, so the regional median would provide a closer proximate of the local 'cost of social inclusion'.

It is worth noting that the UK is made up of four distinct nations which have different degrees of fiscal autonomy. Table

10 shows how poverty lines would change in selected UK regions if they were to secede. The South-East's poverty line would then exceed the North-East's by about a third.

Table 9 **Poverty rates against national and regional poverty lines**

	60% of national median	*60% of regional median*
Italy		
Milan	7.3	14.5
Sicily	46.6	27.3
Spain		
Catalonia	6.7	17.5
Andalusia	27.3	17.9
France		
Greater Paris	10.5	18.7
Calais	23.8	13.9
Ireland		
Dublin	15.0	20.6
West Ireland	25.4	11.5
UK		
South-East England	14.6	20.4
Northern Ireland	29.3	16.9
USA*		
New Jersey*	13.6*	21.8*
Arkansas*	25.7*	14.1*

Note: *Child poverty only; threshold = 50% of respective median
Sources: Statistics gleaned from Kangas and Ritakallio (2004) and Rainwater et al. (2003)

Table 10 **Hypothetical regional poverty lines for a two-adult household in selected UK regions, 2004/05, before housing costs**

	Regional median income	Poverty line	Hypothetical regional poverty line
South-East	£22,300	£12,300	£13,400
London	£21,600	£12,300	£13,000
Scotland	£19,300	£12,300	£11,600
Northern Ireland	£17,700	£12,300	£10,600
Wales	£17,600	£12,300	£10,600
North-East	£17,200	£12,300	£10,300
Total UK	£20,400	£12,300	£12,300

Source: Based on data from Phillips (2008)

To illustrate the effect of a change in boundaries in the other direction (i.e. unifications instead of secessions), Table 11 shows relative poverty rates in three hypothetical countries. These are merely rough-and-ready approximations. They are based on OECD data for income deciles instead of percentiles, so the simplifying assumption was made that, within each decile, the income difference between two adjacent percentiles is constant. These comparisons should therefore be regarded as correct as orders of magnitude. After a merger with Hungary, relative poverty would almost disappear in former Austria and about quadruple in former Hungary. Since Austro-Hungary would be a highly unequal country, the combined RP rate would be very high too. If Sweden and Norway were merged into 'Nordland', relative poverty would fall slightly in Norway and rise notably in Sweden. Unlike its two constituent nations separately, Nordland would not be a uniquely egalitarian country. Merging Spain and Portugal into 'Iberia' results in the Spanish poverty rate falling and in the Portuguese rate rising by about three-quarters.

Table 11 **Poverty rates in three hypothetical countries**

	Median income in PPP-$, 2005	Poverty line in PPP-$ (60% of median income)	Poverty rate
Austria	25,100	15,100	13%
Hungary	9,800	5,900	12%
'Austro-Hungary'	15,700	9,400	26%
Austria as a region of Austro-Hungary	25,100	9,400	3%
Hungary as a region of Austro-Hungary	9,800	9,400	46%
Sweden	20,700	12,400	11%
Norway	26,600	16,000	12%
'Nordland'	22,600	13,600	14%
Sweden as a region of Nordland	20,700	13,600	16%
Norway as a region of Nordland	26,600	16,000	9%
Spain	18,000	10,800	21%
Portugal	12,300	7,400	21%
'Iberia'	16,700	10,000	21%
Spain as a region of Iberia	18,000	10,000	18%
Portugal as a region of Iberia	12,300	10,000	36%

Source: Niemietz (2010a)

Again, all three examples are fully compatible with a relative conception of poverty. The selected countries have either a shared history or mutually intelligible languages, and can hardly be considered entirely separate societies as far as social norms and the concomitant consumption habits are concerned. All of this has, of course, policy implications. If general perceptions of what constitutes adequate living standards depended exclusively on domestic phenomena, then an egalitarian policy which tolerates low growth would appear to have its merits. In contrast, if low earners in Hungary are not as fixated on the domestic median as relative poverty measures would suggest, but rather well aware of consumption habits in neighbouring Austria, then the case for growth-promoting policies that tolerate a widening domestic income distribution is stronger.

On the European level, a poverty rate of 16 per cent (equivalent to a poverty count of 78 million people) is frequently reported (e.g. Caritas Europa, 2010). This rate is an average of 25 or 27 different national poverty rates, measured in relation to 25 or 27 different national median incomes.[1] People in different parts of Europe are increasingly exposed to similar consumption habits and lifestyles, yet we continue to use purely inward-looking domestic relative standards. In the measurement of poverty, we effectively pretend that Hungarians and Czechs are somehow unaware of the much higher living standards in the European West. In the 1960s, when relative measures emerged, it was more plausible than it is today to think of different nations as distinct societies. If European integration has led to a convergence of what are perceived to be acceptable minimal standards of consumption (and it will be shown later that it probably has), the relative approach would be equally compatible with treating Europe as a single country.

Eurostat (2008) provides data on poverty against various thresholds of the pan-European median income of about €1,100 per month for a single person (Table 12). Setting the threshold at 50 per cent would produce a pan-European poverty rate of 16 per cent, about the same as the average of the national poverty rates.[2]

---

1   The inclusion of Romania and Bulgaria does not affect the average of 16 per cent.
2   Set at 60 per cent, the resulting poverty rate of 22.5 per cent would be higher than in any single member state, because pan-Europe would be a highly unequal

Table 12 **Relative poverty in the EU-25, national versus pan-European poverty line(s)**

Poverty line	60% of domestic medians		50% of pan-European median	
Average poverty rate	16%		16%	
	< 10%	> 20%	< 10%	> 60%
	Sweden	Ireland	Slovenia	Lithuania+
	Czech	Greece	Italy	Slovakia+
	Republic	Spain	Cyprus	Latvia+
		Lithuania	Ireland	Hungary+
		Poland	UK*	Poland+
			France*	Estonia+
			Belgium*	
			Germany*	
			Sweden*	
			Netherlands*	
			Finland*	
			Denmark*	
			Austria*	
			Luxembourg*	

Source: Statistics from Eurostat (2008)

But, apart from the average rates, the profiles of the two poverty measures have hardly anything in common. When using domestic medians, almost all countries' poverty rates are clustered in a range between 10 and 20 per cent. In contrast, against the pan-European median, almost all countries display either very low (< 10 per cent) or very high (> 60 per cent) poverty rates. If Europe were a single country, 60 per cent of its poor would live in the new member states, and about a quarter would live in the Mediterranean. Caritas Europa, and others who use the average of the national poverty rates, quote roughly the same figure of 78 million

country. Poverty in the countries marked with a * would still remain below 10 per cent; poverty in the countries marked with a + would rise to above 70 per cent.

Europeans living in poverty as we find from a pan-European measure; the vast majority of 'their' poverty population, however, lives in the EU-15; almost 10 million of them in Germany alone.

UNICEF Innocenti Research Center (2007: 6) argues that 'in today's OECD nations the cutting edge of poverty is the contrast, daily perceived, between the lives of the poor and the lives of those around them'. But unless there is a plausible criterion for deciding who 'those around them' are, the statement is meaningless. There are numerous plausible alternatives to the national level as the domain of poverty assessment, and each one could deliver a fundamentally distinct picture of relative poverty. Economic indicators are usually considered non-robust if a small, plausible change to their definition can fundamentally alter the results. Why should poverty indices be an exception?

'Relative to whom?' The social group question

When using relative measures of poverty, median incomes are taken to be a good approximation of the living standards considered 'typical' in a given territory. The purchasing decisions of median income earners are assumed to define the consumption habits that become 'the norm' in the society in which they live. In this interpretation, the median income earners are, in effect, the standard-setters of social norms. Inability to comply with these standards leads to a state of social exclusion.

Median income should therefore be negatively associated with wellbeing. But again, social wellbeing studies do not always confirm this. Instead of imputing a single standard which others aspire to and try to emulate, social wellbeing studies allow for a multitude of separate or overlapping reference groups. For example, McBride (2001) uses a model in which people benchmark their living standards against those of others in the same age group. Their reference income is given by the average income of their own age group, not by the average of the whole nation.[3] The model has some explanatory power. Falling far behind the living standards of age-mates negatively affects individuals' social wellbeing. The author notes, though, that this benchmarking process is uniform neither over a lifetime nor across the income distribution.

Ferrer-i-Carbonell (2005) defines a more personalised reference group. In her model, people benchmark themselves against others of the same age group who also have a similar education level and live in the same region. Similarly, van de Stadt et al. (1985) define the reference group as people of the same age group, education level and employment status. Clark and Oswald (1996) specify a model in which the comparison group consists of people in the same town, age group, education level, employment category and business sector. Tellingly, each of these model specifications has some explanatory power. There is no single, common reference group that sets the norms for the whole of society. People in different circumstances differ in the living standards and consumption habits they consider 'the norm', and the cost of social inclusion varies with personal circumstances as well.

Differences between the norms of social subgroups, and the cost of participating in them, are only the tip of the iceberg. Fafchamps and Shilpi (2008) show that the process of reference group formation is not uniform within a country or over time. It

---

3   The age group is defined as the respondent's age +/– five years.

varies with the extent to which a locality is integrated into wider patterns of market exchange, and thus with exposure to geographically distant people's lifestyles. The intensity of benchmarking against a reference standard also varies with the composition of the consumption basket. For some goods, respondents' perceptions of what constituted acceptable standards depended a lot on what was available to others around them. For other goods, respondents were rather indifferent to what others had. For example, most respondents tolerated differences in the standard of clothing, but not in the standard of healthcare.

In short, there is no reason why the cost of social inclusion should be a fixed fraction of median income or, more generally, why median income earners should be the standard-setters of social norms. Relative poverty measures emerged in a time when overall living standards were considerably lower than today and the scope for differentiated consumption habits was, arguably, smaller. It was easier than today to define a 'mainstream society' with a characteristic pattern of consumption – a car, a television, a radio, etc. Townsend and Abel-Smith realised that while ownership of these items was not necessary for survival, falling very far behind this standard set people apart from the rest of society. But in today's context, the concept of a mainstream consumption pattern that everybody tries to emulate seems outdated.

The absence of a universal concept of a 'normal' living standard and of a generic reference income has policy implications. Almost all social wellbeing studies suggest that people care about how they compare relative to others – but they do not suggest that people care about nothing else. People are interested in both their absolute and their relative standing. Providing the conditions under which people can fulfil the first objective is a feasible policy objective. Bringing people's income closer to that of some highly subjective, unobservable peer group is not: even less so if there is a disconnect between perceived inequalities and actual inequalities, as seems to be the case. The Institute for Fiscal Studies reports that 'IFS maintains a website (http://www.ifs.org. uk/wheredoyoufitin/) allowing individuals to calculate where they lie in the income distribution. Most users are surprised to discover how far up the income distribution they really are' (Brewer et al., 2008a: 25). A qualitative study by the Institute for Social and Economic Research also finds that:

> People may have some sense of a large disparity between top earners and people 'at the bottom', but they are not necessarily well informed about particular occupational incomes. Not only this, we have to ask how likely it is that they would necessarily be aware of incomes even among those known to them personally. (Pahl et al., 2007: 6)

In any case, most studies on subjective wellbeing (SWB) suggest that people are much more interested in how they compare with peers with similar socioeconomic characteristics rather than to some abstract national average. This means that people within a benchmark group will often be in the same tax bracket, or qualify for the same benefits, so that traditional redistributive instruments will hardly affect within-group income distances.

On the whole, compressing the national income distribution in the hope of bringing people closer to some unobservable, highly individualised peer group is like bombarding a village in the hope of hitting a group of terrorists who are known to be hiding there. Some of the bombs will certainly strike terrorists. But there will be heavy casualties, and most terrorists will escape unscathed anyway.

'Relative to when?' The intertemporal dimension

Relative poverty standards count increases in average living standards against material gains enjoyed by the poor, on the grounds that these increases raise consumption-related norms. Crucially, they also treat this offsetting as taking effect instantaneously. A sudden increase in median incomes in conjunction with a smaller proportionate increase in the incomes of the poor is likely to lead to an increase in poverty. This is the case even if the increase in the incomes of the better off is spent on what might be regarded, at least for a time, as luxuries, and the increase in the incomes of the poor allows them to obtain basic goods such as fuel and housing. Relative measures ignore the dimension of *time* in the formation of norms and expectations. What we perceive as a normal standard of living is treated exclusively as a function of the standards we *presently* see around us, with no reference either to what we experienced in the recent past, or what we expect to experience in the near future.

The experience of Ireland during its high-growth period is a case study which reveals the limited nature of this approach and which has puzzled many adherents of relative poverty measures. UNICEF Innocenti Research Center (2005: 7) notes: 'In the 1990s ... Ireland saw sustained economic growth that brought a near doubling of average incomes. Clearly, child poverty has in one sense been reduced. But relative poverty remained largely unchanged.' Hills (2004: 42) explains this phenomenon, which he labels the 'Irish Paradox', as follows: 'The poor were a lot better off in real terms than they had been, but relative poverty still rose. This jarred with public perceptions of what poverty constituted, since it had not adjusted upwards as fast as average living standards.'

Supporters of relative measures ignore the factor of time. Callan et al. (1998), for example, state: '*over time*, increases in general living standards will come to be fully reflected in expectations about what is sufficient to participate fully in society' (emphasis added), but omit the fact that this is precisely not what relative poverty figures measure. They do not allow for a time lag that has to elapse before a rise in overall living standards has translated into changed perceptions of what is a 'typical' lifestyle. If they did, they would have to distinguish between societies that record similar living standards at present, but which have reached their current positions through different time trajectories (e.g. Switzerland, Singapore and Iceland).

It would be entirely coherent *within* the relative poverty framework to adopt a notion of 'intertemporal relativity'. Living standards would be put in context, yet that context would consist not only of other people's present income, but also of other people's and each agent's own past income. In this version of relative poverty, the income distribution at a single point in time would become less important, because rapid improvements in living standards would outweigh 'snapshot inequalities'.

Table 13 illustrates this for two hypothetical societies, 'Growthland' and 'Egalitaria',[4] which start with identical median incomes in year 0. Incomes grow across the board at a constant annual rate, which is 5 per cent in Growthland and 1 per cent in Egalitaria. There is no change in the income distribution recorded at any single point in time, and no social mobility. The two societies are unaware of one another; consumption-related norms are formed exclusively at the domestic level.

---

4   The names are borrowed from Myddelton (1994: 35–7).

Table 13 **The evolution of incomes in Growthland and Egalitaria**

Year	Incomes in Growthland		Incomes in Egalitaria	
	Poor	Middle class	Poor	Middle class
0	45.0	100.0	65.0	100.0
1	47.7	105.0	65.7	101.0
2	49.6	110.3	66.3	102.0
3	52.1	115.8	67.0	103.0
...	...	...	...	...
10	73.3	162.9	71.8	110.5
...	...	...	...	...
17	103.1	229.2	77.0	118.4
...	...	...	...	...
44	385.1	855.7	100.7	154.9

The poor in Growthland are always farther behind their domestic middle class than the poor in Egalitaria. But they are always closer to where the domestic middle class was ten years earlier, and they always compare better relative to their own past income than the poor in Egalitaria. In Growthland, the incomes of the poor will have reached today's median incomes in 17 years, a process which will take 44 years in Egalitaria. Egalitaria is more 'snapshot egalitarian', while Growthland is more 'intertemporarily egalitarian' over a longer time horizon.

During its high-growth period, Ireland was the next-best thing to Growthland. For example, the incomes of the second-poorest decile in the mid-2000s and the incomes of the next-higher decile in the late 1990s are very similar. Ireland had become a much more unequal society in a snapshot perspective, but a much more egalitarian society in an intertemporal perspective.

Table 14 'Intertemporal inequality' in Ireland: average income of
decile 'i' compared with the average income of decile 'i+1'
five years earlier

2004		1999	
Decile	Weekly income	Decile	Weekly income
1	€159	2	€174
2	€245	3	€249
3	€359	4	€331

Source: Data from Central Statistics Office Ireland (2007: 15)

The injection of the time dimension into the relative poverty framework has policy implications, because the Irish experience was not merely a 'special case', in the sense of a rare, random occurrence. Ireland's experience resulted from deliberately adopted pro-growth policies (see Edwards and Mitchell, 2008: 36; Heath, 2006: 38, 67–71; and Fraser Institute, 2009: 112). There is no reason why the UK economy should not be able to grow at Irish rates.

In 1992, equivalised real incomes in the UK were £633 per month for the 10th percentile, and £1,387 for the 50th percentile.[5] By 2008, these figures had increased to £870 and £1,765 respectively. If, instead, all UK incomes had grown at a constant rate equal to Ireland's long-term average growth rate,[6] then the 10th percentile would have reached £1,493 and the 50th percentile £3,122. That is, under the 'alternative history' scenario, real incomes of the 'poor' in 2008 would have been above the level of

5   In 2008 prices, based on data from Institute for Fiscal Studies (2010).
6   The average annual growth rate of real GDP per capita in Ireland between 1975 and 2004 is 5.2 per cent. To avoid an unrealistically high figure, the long-run average is taken, instead of importing the Irish growth rates of the same 1990–2006 period.

median incomes in the early 1990s. It is simply implausible that consumption-related social norms could have adjusted upwards so quickly that the poor would have perceived themselves as having gained nothing from this. When growth rates are high, relative indicators become increasingly less realistic approximations of social realities because, even if the benchmark by which people consider themselves having sufficient to participate fully in society rises, the incomes of the poor just run ahead of them. Notably, this point is indirectly conceded even in *The Spirit Level*, probably the most widely quoted defence of egalitarianism in recent years. The authors note that inequality becomes less important when growth is rapid and argue that, by implication, inequality is incompatible with their ultimate goal of an economy without growth: 'It is not simply that growth is a substitute for equality, it is that greater equality makes growth much less necessary. It is a precondition for a steady-state economy [by which they mean a zero-growth economy]' (Wilkinson and Pickett, 2009: 221–2).

The policies that would lead to a rapid economic expansion should be considered a valid option for anti-poverty policies. Snapshot-relative poverty measures, however, are grossly biased against such a strategy. In poverty studies that compare the recent evolution of relative poverty rates across wealthy nations, Ireland usually comes out with the largest percentage point increase (Scruggs and Allan, 2006: 884; OECD, 2008: 129; Smeeding, 2006: 78). And under the 'alternative history' scenario of all UK incomes growing at the long-term Irish rate between 1992 and 2008, relative poverty in 2008 would have been higher than it actually was.

How relative is relative enough?

Defenders of relative measures of poverty argue that the cost of social participation rises with overall living standards. It has been argued here that, on an abstract level, this is convincing. Such defenders, however, provide no reason for the assertion, implicit in conventional relative poverty measures, that average living standards and the cost of social participation should rise *by the same proportion*. Under conventional relative poverty measures, the poverty line is a fixed fraction of median incomes, so if the latter rise by p per cent, then the poverty line rises by the same p per cent, and the so-called 'income elasticity of the poverty line' (IEP) with regard to median income is equal to 1.

There is little research on how to determine a plausible figure for the IEP: the relationship between the cost of social participation and median incomes. One of the rare examples is the 'Leyden Poverty Line' (see Wolff, 2009: 96–9). It is derived from the survey data used to produce a majoritarian subjective poverty line. Households are asked what they consider the minimum amount needed to live a decent life in their society. These responses are plotted against the respondents' income. For US data, that gradient amounts to 0.6: if people's income increases by 1 per cent, their perception of what constitutes a necessary minimum amount increases by 0.6 per cent. The Leyden researchers interpret this gradient as an appropriate IEP.

Madden (2000) uses a similar logic, but looks at actual purchasing decisions instead of relying on people's survey responses. He derives the income elasticity of demand – the responsiveness of demand for a product to changes in income

Figure 7 **The evolution of the weekly UK poverty line for a two-adult household under different income elasticities of the poverty line (IEP) from 1962 onwards**
£, 1961–2006 (2006 prices)

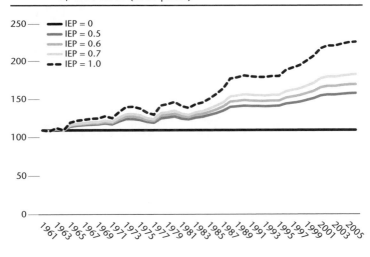

Source: Based on data from Institute for Fiscal Studies (2007)

– for several necessities.[7] The average of these income elasticities is interpreted as an income elasticity of the poverty line. The author finds an IEP between 0.5 and 0.7. Both approaches suggest that the appropriate IEP should be somewhere in between the IEP of conventional relative and absolute indicators, which are equal to 1 and 0 respectively.

Figure 7 shows how the poverty line (for a two-adult household) in the UK would have developed over time using alternative

---

7   The 'necessities' are taken from a material deprivation index; spending data come from a large-scale expenditure survey.

Figure 8   UK poverty rates in 2006, when updating the poverty line with alternative income elasticities from 1962 onwards

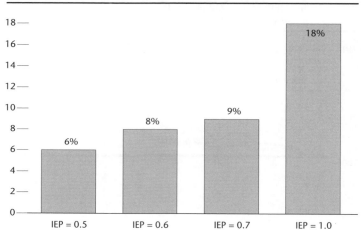

Source: Based on data from Muriel (2008)

IEPs. The starting point is the poverty line of the year 1961, as 60 per cent of the median income in 1961. From 1962 on, the poverty line is adjusted each year by the growth in median income, multiplied by the IEP.

Again, a different uprating mechanism for the poverty line is entirely consistent with a relative framework. All the poverty lines shown in Figure 7 are relative ones that are coupled to median incomes. Over time, the way in which the poverty line is uprated makes a substantial difference. Figure 8 shows the poverty rates that would have resulted for the UK in 2006 under different uprating regimes for the poverty line. Poverty rates would have been substantially lower than the 18 per cent actually observed in that year.

Small, and quite plausible, changes in the poverty definition lead to substantially different results. One may, of course, consider the IEP values used here as far-fetched or arbitrary. But an IEP of unity is arbitrary too. Even within the relative poverty framework, there is no reason why any increase in median incomes should translate one for one into higher social participation costs. If the IEP is less than unity, countries can eventually grow out of poverty without changes in the income distribution.

Über-relativism and the anti-growth ideology

More recently, a number of authors have taken the relative view of wealth and poverty a step farther (see Wilkinson and Pickett, 2009; Coote et al., 2010; Simms et al., 2010; Woodward and Simms, 2006; Layard, 2005; Frank, 1999). Within the traditional relative poverty perspective, the effect of growth in absolute living standards is an ambiguous one. Growth can relieve material hardship, but it can also impose higher social integration costs on people. Proponents of this perspective do not see growth as an important issue, but they have never been 'opposed' to growth. Proponents of the *über*-relativist perspective, in contrast, believe that growth is only conducive to wellbeing and social progress at low levels of economic development:

> One of the central findings of the large scientific literature
> on subjective well-being is that once income levels surpass
> a minimal absolute threshold, average satisfaction levels
> within a given country tend to be highly stable over time,
> even in the face of significant economic growth. (Frank,
> 1999: 72)

The fact that growth still occurs beyond this saturation point is seen as the result of a market failure of sorts: when people make efforts to improve their income situation, what they are really trying to achieve is not to make themselves better off in absolute terms, but to make themselves better off relative to others. In this perspective, growth really is a zero-sum game:

> When I earn more and adopt a more expensive lifestyle, this puts pressure on others to keep up – my action raises the norm and makes them less satisfied with what they have. I am like the factory owner who pours out his soot on to the neighbours' laundry. And the classic economic remedy for pollution is to make the polluters pay. (Layard, 2005: 15–16)

Income growth beyond the saturation point, it is argued, is channelled into the acquisition of 'positional goods' – goods which are acquired not for their value in use, but to express a social standing relative to others. This makes the pursuit of growth a pointless tilt at windmills. The value of a positional good derives solely from the fact that other people do not possess it. If the prevalence of a positional good increases, it becomes less valuable to those who already possess it. Growth becomes a 'prisoners' dilemma'-type coordination failure; the result of behaviour which is rational from an individual but irrational from a collective perspective:

> If an important part of consumerism is driven by emulation, status competition, or simply having to run to keep up with everyone else, and is basically about social appearances and position, this would explain why we continue to pursue economic growth despite its apparent lack of benefits. If everyone wants more money because it improves self-image and status in relation to others, then each person's desire to be richer does not add up to a societal desire for economic growth. (Ibid.: 224–5)

Hence, in the *über*-relativist perspective, growth is not simply a less important issue, but a social failure which has to be actively and forcibly restricted.

One problem with this interpretation is that its proponents quote subjective wellbeing research (SWB) in an extremely selective way.[8] There are contradictory findings on the relative importance of relative and absolute income levels for social wellbeing. Stevenson and Wolfers (2008) argue that the failure to find a significant association between absolute income levels and self-reported happiness – the so-called 'Easterlin Paradox' – merely reflects insufficient and inadequate data in earlier SWB studies. Repeating the exercise with more recent data sets, they find a significant and robust association between SWB and absolute living standards even at very high levels of economic development. Summarising several empirical studies with similar findings, Lane (1993) even goes a step farther, arguing that 'new studies have almost completely reversed Easterlin's conclusions. These studies have found that economic growth does materially increase a country's collective sense of well-being and that differences in well-being within a country are not significantly related to income.'

This lends no support to the narrative of growth as a vicious trap which nobody actually wants, but from which people cannot liberate themselves without external help. The empirical observation that annual working hours per employee show a long-term downward trend is also difficult to reconcile with this narrative

8   Whether or not SWB studies are the appropriate tool for long-term time-series studies involving correlations with GDP is beyond the scope of this monograph. Johns and Ormerod (2007: 82–3) show that they are not: SWB is measured within a fixed scale, say 1–3 or 1–10. GDP, in contrast, can grow indefinitely.

(Niemietz, 2010b). Growth opponents assert that the primary (if not the sole) purpose of consumption that goes beyond the acquisition of necessities is status-signalling. But the spending of typical consumers does not follow a pattern that one would expect under this hypothesis. Highly visible consumption, which *might* serve a status-signalling function (people's 'true' motivation cannot be known), represents only a small share of an average consumer's budget. Most spending is either barely visible to others, or wholly inappropriate for status-signalling (see Table 15).

Table 15 **Highly and barely visible consumption of average households**

	Annual expenditure	% of annual budget
Highly visible consumption		
Jewellery, clocks, watches and other personal effects	£109	0.4%
Hairdressing, beauty treatment, hair products, cosmetics and related accessories	£328	1.3%
Outer garments	£754	3.1%
Barely visible consumption		
Transport services excluding air fares	£452	1.8%
Insurance	£759	3.1%
Food and drinks consumed at home	£3,162	12.9%

Source: Based on data from the Office for National Statistics (2010a)

This is not to say that policymakers should actively 'promote' growth through, for example, artificially encouraging high levels of savings. But they should not coercively restrain growth. Markets frequently do overcome coordination failures. If it is true that growth merely amounts to a pointless status race, then nothing in a market economy can stop people from forming voluntary groups which opt out of the status race to embrace non-materialistic lifestyles, values and reward systems. Competition between different sets of values, instead of a grand, government-imposed scheme, would then produce the 'optimal' mix through trial and error.

Misuses of relative poverty figures

Proponents of relative measures of poverty were correct in arguing that poverty must be understood within a context of prevailing social norms, compliance with which comes at a cost. But setting the poverty line as a fixed fraction of the contemporary national average income does not translate this idea into a sensible measure. A measure of inequality (in the bottom half of the distribution) is not the same as a measure of social participation, and there are a variety of reasons for keeping the two apart.

First of all, it is not true that proponents of relative measures 'confuse' poverty with inequality, as their critics often claim. Within their set of assumptions, poverty *is* inequality. In the policy debate, however, relative poverty rates are not presented in these terms. They are not presented as the rates resulting from one very particular definition, based on very restrictive assumptions. Instead, the figure produced by this measure is usually simply presented as 'the number of people living below the poverty line' or 'the number of people living in poverty'. Worse still, it is very common to combine the rates resulting from one poverty definition with the interpretation belonging to a different definition. A case in point is the current 'Zero Poverty' campaign by Caritas Europa (2010), which claims: 'Around 78 million people in the 27 EU member states (16% of the total population) ... live on or below the poverty line. They often lack money for the bare essentials such as fuel for heating, clothing and minor repairs.'

The figure of 78 million or 16 per cent belongs to a relative definition, while the interpretation would correctly belong either to a material deprivation index, or to some absolute measure based on the cost of the mentioned items. The combination is invalid because the relative definition to which the figures belong does not convey information about which goods people cannot afford, nor was it designed to this end. The same applies to Save the Children's (n.d.) statement that 'in the UK, 3.9 million children live in poverty. Many don't have access to warm winter clothing, nutritious food, decent housing or education.' It may, of course, be true that many of those living in relative poverty do not have access to such things, but the relative poverty figures tell us absolutely nothing about the extent to which this is so. Hard data from one measure are being used to imply something about a measure for which these particular data reveal nothing.

A more subtle version of the same confounding can be found in the 2010 edition of Caritas Switzerland's (2010) *Sozialalmanach*. A chapter on various estimates of relative poverty in Switzerland (pp. 101–14) is followed by six interviews with poor people, describing the specific deprivations they face in their daily lives (pp. 115–28). If the purpose of this sequence is to make the figures come alive through anecdotes, then it fails in this task. The experiences of these six people would have been an apt illustration of material deprivation figures, or of absolute poverty figures with a meaningful interpretation. Or else, to link relative poverty figures to stories, Caritas Switzerland could have included anecdotes from people who can easily afford key necessities, but who frequently have to abstain from activities that most people around them can undertake, and who therefore feel a sense of social exclusion. Again, detailed research about a concept which is easy to measure is being used, in this case illustrated by the experiences of a very small number of people, to make a point about an entirely different concept.

A conceptual error of a similar type is committed in statements that attempt to contrast relative poverty rates with a country's absolute level of wealth or income or with the growth of wealth or income. End Child Poverty (n.d.), for example, notes that '4 million children – one in three – are currently living in poverty in the UK, one of the highest rates in the industrialised world. This is a shocking figure given the wealth of our nation.' Oxfam Great Britain (n.d.) comments: 'The UK is the fifth richest country in the world. Until the recession hit in 2008, it had experienced an unprecedented period of growth over the last 10 years. Yet this has not benefited the poorest in society.'

Statements such as these imply that high poverty rates would be pardonable in a poor country but not in a rich one; that there ought to be an inverse relationship between a nation's absolute wealth and its poverty rate. This claim would be perfectly valid for a material deprivation or an absolute poverty index. But relative rates are not related to GDP or growth rates, nor were they ever meant to be. Confounding two distinct concepts deprives both of their meaning. It conveys the systematically wrong impression that economic progress had no impact on the quantity and quality of goods and services that people at the bottom end of the income distribution can afford. This fallacy is repeated in the often heard claim that the present economic downturn has made it harder for the government to reach the main child poverty target. It has not. If anything, the crisis has made it easier by reducing the incomes of the better off! Relative poverty in the UK fell during the recessions of the mid-1970s, the early 1980s and the early 1990s (Muriel and Sibieta, 2009: 27–34). Median incomes fell, and the poverty line followed suit, while benefits and pensions remained constant in real terms.

An even more obvious version of the fallacy of confounding distinct poverty concepts is presented by the Child Poverty Action Group (2009), which finds: 'international evidence [shows] that income inequality and poverty are very closely linked' (ibid.: 17), and illustrates this by plotting OECD countries' relative poverty rates against Gini-coefficients. They effectively define poverty as inequality, and then go on to 'demonstrate' that poverty is highly correlated to inequality.[9]

The relative measure of poverty jars with the way a majority in Britain understands the term 'poverty'. According to the British Social Attitude survey, only 22 per cent of respondents subscribed to the definition that someone in Britain was poor when 'they had enough to buy the things they really needed, but not enough to buy the things that most people take for granted'. However, 50 per cent agreed that someone in Britain was in poverty when 'they had enough to eat and live, but not enough to buy other things they needed' (Sefton, 2009: 227).

One serious problem with relative poverty measures is that a commitment to minimising inequality cannot be an element of a free society. In a heterogeneous society, people differ immensely in their values and the goals they choose in life, in the trade-offs

9   The two measures do not capture precisely the same phenomenon. RP based on the median measures inequality in the bottom half of the distribution; the Gini-coefficient is based on the whole income distribution and gives especial weight to the middle.

they make between their several goals, and the strategies they choose to put them into practice. This involves different trade-offs between wealth and non-material aims, such as leisure, a fulfilled social life and spiritual fulfilment. It involves different attitudes towards entrepreneurship, risk-taking, work, education or thrift; and different strategies for achieving these ends. Such differences will inevitably lead to vast differences in economic outcomes. It is inconsistent to uphold the principle of personal autonomy in making vastly different choices in life, but to oppose the resulting differences in economic outcomes. Suppose the electorate could somehow agree on an optimal level of inequality and on the means to achieve it. Individual preferences that deviate from the norm – e.g. an exceptionally high, or an exceptionally low, preference for material wealth – would then pose a 'threat' to the envisaged inequality target. The logical correlate of the position that 'what matters is the level of inequality you finish up with, not how you get it' (Wilkinson and Pickett, 2009: 237) would be government restrictions of career choices and lifestyle choices. This can be illustrated by two contemporary real-world examples:

1. One of the reasons, though not the major one, why inequality and relative poverty in the UK increased in the 1980s was an increase in self-employment (Brewer et al., 2009b: 19). Summary measures of inequality among the self-employed (i.e. the inequality measure that would result if the self-employed formed a separate society) are always higher than for other occupational groups (ibid.: 84). An increase in overall inequality can either result from an increase in inequality within an occupational group, or from compositional changes, i.e. by people switching from a low-

inequality to a high-inequality group. Yet few would argue that the government should prevent people from entering into particular occupational sectors, or tax any income differences between sectors away. An 'inequality target' taken seriously would require such decisions.

2. Between the mid-1980s and the mid-1990s, the Netherlands recorded one of the sharpest increases in relative poverty in the developed world. The rapid employment creation of this period was a contributing factor, because the improved job opportunities were often taken up by previously non-working partners in middle-class households. Thus, the rise in the share of dual-earner households was more pronounced among the better off than among the less well off, driving household incomes further apart (Marx, 2007). To the extent that these decisions reflect different trade-offs between consumption and leisure, however, it would be difficult to argue against this development.[10] In order to maintain the income distribution of the status quo ante, the government would either have to levy tax rates of close to 100 per cent on second earners in wealthy households, or nudge the non-working partners in poorer single breadwinner families into employment.

None of this means that a free society *must* be an unequal society. In traditional, more homogeneous societies, low or moderate levels of inequality can result without the employment

---

10   There is disagreement about the extent to which this was actually the case – Marx (2007) argues that the employment opportunities available to the poor had been overestimated. But he does not express an objection to the rising inequality insofar as it reflected voluntary decisions.

Figure 9   **Gini-coefficients of disposable income (DI) or market income (MI) [black bars] in selected OECD countries**

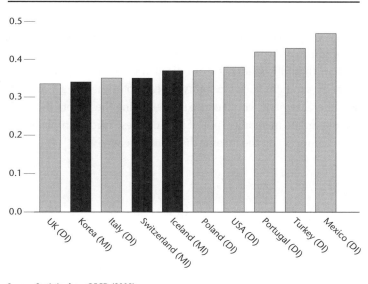

Source: Statistics from OECD (2008)

of coercive means. In South Korea and Switzerland, inequalities before taxes and transfers (i.e. of market income) are moderate, and smaller than US inequalities after taxes and transfers (i.e. of disposable income) (Figure 9).

More importantly, there are numerous drivers of inequality which are no less incompatible with the principles of a free society. The assertion that classical liberalism was 'in favour' of inequality (e.g. Lawlor et al., 2009: 9–10) is a complete misrepresentation. Anti-liberal drivers of inequality include the following: entry barriers to the labour market (including particular markets such as the taxi market) and to self-employment; government spending on services that are disproportionately used by the wealthy (such as art subsidies); regressive taxes; trade restrictions; supply-side restrictions and regulations that raise the cost of products on which the poor particularly rely; and an education system that fails students from disadvantaged backgrounds and thereby dampens social mobility. In each of these cases, however, the liberal remedy would consist of removing the factors that artificially inflate inequality, not of leaving these factors in place and then compressing the income distribution coercively.

9 THE FLAWS OF INCOME-BASED POVERTY MEASURES

Thus far, the terms 'incomes' and 'living standards' have been used as synonyms: our discussion of poverty has centred on the incomes that people receive. In reality, the correlation between income and other measures of living standards is not particularly high towards the bottom of the distribution of incomes; this correlation has become lower over time. For families with children, Brewer et al. (2009a) have plotted income against more direct measures of living standards, such as household expenditure, possession of consumer durables, material deprivation, and cash-flow problems. Income could be considered a fair predictor of living standards if:

1. two households with identical incomes experienced similar living standards (or deprivation) on other measures; and if
2. direct measures of living standards rose linearly (and direct measures of deprivation fell linearly) with income.

In the lower half of the distribution, neither condition holds. There is a considerable spread in living standards for any given level of income. Households with identical incomes can experience vastly different living standards. On average, the relationship between the two is not a linear but a roughly U-shaped one. Starting in the middle of the income distribution and moving downwards, living standards fall initially, as one should expect. But approaching the very bottom, living standards *rise* again (ibid.: 69–84). Living standards are at their lowest when incomes are between 30 and 50 per cent of the median – they then rise as incomes fall below that range. On average, households with incomes very far below the income poverty line experience much higher living standards than households closer to it.

This does not mean that income data are uninformative. It is only at the very bottom of the income distribution that income and other living standards measures fall apart completely. But it does make the common poverty line of 60 per cent of median income a crude instrument for identifying those with the lowest living standards. Measures of extreme relative poverty – that is those below 40 per cent of median income – are particularly inappropriate. Some of those not included by this measure experience lower living standards than many of those who are included. What explains the mismatch?

Income as an incomplete snapshot

Income is subject to fluctuations over time, so a household's recorded income at a given point in time need not be representative of that household's 'typical' income situation. This is particularly obvious for the self-employed and freelance workers, whose income streams are the most uneven ones and can be negative at times. Employees' income, too, can be temporarily elevated owing to bonus payments, paid overtime or a temporary additional income source; or temporarily depressed owing to short-term unemployment, a short-term reduction in working hours, parental leave, or a period of retraining. Indeed, very high earners will often take career breaks during which they may be paid nothing but live off their capital.

This makes income poverty statistics sensitive to the accounting period chosen. The standard accounting period is the calendar year or the fiscal year, but this is merely an arbitrary convention. There is no particular reason why a biannual period should be too long or a semi-annual one too short. Wolff (2009: 121–2) reviews various studies that experiment with alternative period lengths in the US context. A consistent finding is that the shorter the accounting period, the higher the poverty rate. If poverty statistics were based on monthly instead of annual income, the poverty rate would rise by almost a quarter. The difference is explained by people whose income falls below the poverty line for some months, but not for long enough to pull their annual average income below the poverty line. Conversely, longer accounting periods lead to lower poverty rates. The difference is explained by people who experience a low-income spell which is long enough to pull their annual average income of a single year below the poverty line, but not long enough to pull down a longer-term average. Temporary income losses are offset by subsequent or previous higher-income periods.

Unless averaged over a long period, income-based measures are characterised by an inherent 'anti-volatility-bias'. The self-employed, for example, are identified as a high-risk group in income-based poverty statistics (e.g. Sutherland et al., 2003: 14). Median incomes among the self-employed are higher than median incomes among the salaried – but they are also more volatile, so at any given point in time, the proportion recording an income below the poverty line is higher among the self-employed than among the salaried. The same anti-volatility bias applies to whole economies. When comparing a dynamic economy with a high share of self-employment and flexible labour markets, with an economy with a large public sector and a rigid labour market, an income-based measure will, other things being equal, identify the first economy to be more poverty prone. Since income volatility within a given economy is not constant over time, the same bias is present in within-country comparisons over time.

Yet since Friedman (1957) established the 'Permanent Income Hypothesis', it has become well documented that living standards do not fluctuate by the same magnitude as incomes. People tend to smooth their consumption by building up savings and assets in periods when their income is above the expected long-term average, and drawing on them in periods when it is below.

According to the Permanent Income Hypothesis, *expenditure* is close to expected long-term average income. It is therefore less sensitive to the choice of the accounting period than income.

Expenditure measures have drawbacks of their own. Detailed, interview-based expenditure surveys are more complicated to undertake and not nearly as widely available as income data. They also suffer from the fact that stated preferences do not always coincide with revealed preferences. The accuracy of expenditure survey figures can be judged by checking whether they gross up to the National Account figures, i.e. by checking whether what people profess to buy matches what is actually being bought and sold in the country recorded in other ways. For socially 'stigmatised' items, a large gap between the two can be observed. In the UK, only half of the recorded alcohol and tobacco sales volumes show up in the Expenditure and Food Survey (EFS), recently renamed the Living Cost and Food Survey (LCF) (Attanasio et al., 2006: 36–8). Apart from deliberate under-reporting, expenditure surveys are also likely to suffer from random inaccuracies, since some of the expenditure questions refer to a longer time horizon.

Overall, however, aggregate reported spending mirrored National Account figures fairly well until quite recently. Until the mid-1990s, aggregating what people reported they bought explained well over 90 per cent of what was officially being sold; from that point on, the proportion has fallen to about 80 per cent (ibid.: 31–3).

Income data, however, suffer from similar and probably greater shortcomings. Income poverty statistics are also based on large-scale surveys, such as the Family Resources Survey (FRS) in the UK. Just as people under-report spending on particular items, they under-report income from particular sources. The amount of money people profess to receive in benefits does not gross up to the amount of money that, according to administrative data, is being paid out. For many benefit categories, both the number of recipients and the amount paid out per recipient do not match official data. Only about two-thirds of the amount the Department for Work and Pensions pays out in tax credits and pension credits shows up in the FRS (Brewer et al., 2008a: 87–93).[1] Indeed, misrecording of benefit incomes is a likely contributor to the mentioned mismatch between income and other measures of living standards. Brewer et al. (2009a: 117–47) also show that while the mismatch is somewhat rectified by taking the duration of low-income spells into account, it by no means disappears. There are households reporting low incomes for extended periods which nevertheless do not seem to experience material hardship.

---

1   The exact proportion fluctuates from year to year, suggesting that deliberate under-reporting is probably not the only reason for the mismatch. There seem to be genuine misunderstandings concerning the benefits system.

In short, while an imperfect solution, there is a strong case for basing poverty statistics on expenditure instead of income data. Would this make a large difference to recorded poverty? For earlier decades, it may not. Goodman and Webb (1995) show that by the late 1970s, a household's income was still a reasonable predictor of its expenditure, albeit by no means a perfect one. But, from then on, the spread between 'high spenders' and 'low spenders' widened within all income deciles, and it widened most in the top and the bottom decile. At least for these two deciles, income has become a poor predictor of spending and therefore of the living standards of the poor.

The authors also show how the composition of the bottom decile has changed. Income deciles or quintiles are, as Myddelton (1994: 35) put it, 'like a hotel with some "permanent" but many transient residents'. In these terms, the bottom income decile is a hotel which has changed its booking policies to a greater extent than other decile hotels since the late 1970s. The share of pensioners in this decile, a group with a rather stable income situation, has fallen by more than half.

Poverty narratives: income versus expenditure

Having recapitulated the advantages of spending data over income data, it is worthwhile describing how a poverty analysis based on spending data would look for the UK context. While this is not the common approach, time series data for the level and distribution of spending are nevertheless available (see Goodman and Webb, 1995; Blow et al., 2004; Brewer et al., 2006a; Leicester, 2006, Blundell and Etheridge, 2008). Median equivalised spending shows, unsurprisingly, the same long-term trend as median equivalised income. Also, both have become more unequal over time. But the magnitude and the timing of the increases in inequality differ. Leicester (2006) provides data on 'relative expenditure poverty' where households are classified as poor when their expenditure falls below 60 per cent of median expenditure. Relative expenditure poverty is, of course, just as unconvincing a concept as relative income poverty, because all the flaws of the latter apply to the former. But what these figures provide is a hint about which poverty narrative would prevail today if poverty statistics had always been based on expenditure data, with everything else held constant.

Figure 10 shows that, under these circumstances, the conventional wisdom on poverty could not have arisen. In fact, relative expenditure poverty supports no narrative at all. It is neither trendless in the 1970s, nor does it suddenly explode in the 1980s, stagnate in the early 1990s, or turn around in the late 1990s. Instead, it describes an almost linear upward trend that begins in the 1970s, and which flattened out only recently. Figure 10 also shows a measure of long-term relative income poverty, the share of households that fell below the relative poverty line in at least three out of the last four years (only available from 1994 onwards). This measure merely seems to parallel the pattern of the snapshot measure at a lower level, suggesting that the shortcomings of income data cannot be removed by merely extending the accounting period.

Changing from income to expenditure also changes the impression about how absolute living standards at the bottom have evolved over time. The evolution of the bottom decile's income differs markedly across different periods, with a prolonged fall in the 1980s and a considerable increase between

Figure 10 **Relative income poverty, relative expenditure poverty and persistent relative income poverty, 1974–2005**

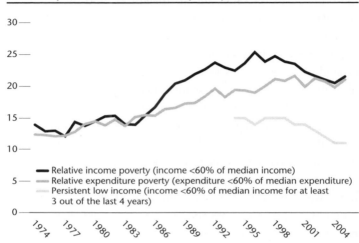

Sources: Statistics from Institute for Fiscal Studies (2008); Leicester (2006); Office for National Statistics and Department for Work and Pensions (2009a)

the mid-1990s and the early 2000s (see Figure 11). The evolution of the bottom decile's expenditure shows no such swings, but evolves much more steadily over time.

Income data thus exaggerate the inequality explosion of the 1980s. Blundell and Etheridge (2008) decompose the distributional changes that occurred during this period into the changes in hourly gross wages, gross income, household income, disposable income and finally consumption. They show that the *early* 1980s were indeed characterised by large and lasting increases in wage inequality, driven mainly by increases in education differentials and experience differentials. There was also an increase

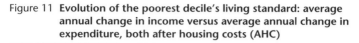

Figure 11 **Evolution of the poorest decile's living standard: average annual change in income versus average annual change in expenditure, both after housing costs (AHC)**

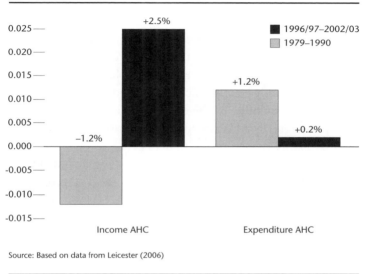

Source: Based on data from Leicester (2006)

in long-term, entrenched worklessness among the low-skilled, which must have contributed to long-term inequality. But what happened later in the same decade had large transitory components which did not feed through into consumption inequality.

A similar difference in 'poverty narratives' is obtained for the USA. The official income-based absolute measure tells a puzzling tale of a decade-long stagnation of poverty, amid strong economic growth and labour market performance. The impression is that at some point in recent history, the economy has decoupled the poor from overall progress. Journal articles with titles such as 'Why has economic growth been such an ineffective tool against poverty in recent years?' and 'Poverty, income distribution and growth: are they still connected?' abound (see Blank, 1996; Blank and Card, 1993; DeFina, 2002).

Eberstadt (2007), however, shows a grave mismatch between income figures and other measures of living standards for the poor. In particular, towards the bottom of the distribution, income and expenditure have diverged. In the early 1960s, income was a fairly good predictor of expenditure of households in the bottom quintile. By the early 1970s, a gap of 40 per cent had opened, and by 2004 average expenditure in this quintile was twice as high as average income (ibid.: 19).

More specifically, Meyer and Sullivan (2007) show that if poverty figures were based on expenditure instead of income, the poverty rate would have fallen substantially between 1980 and 2004. Needless to say, this does not mean that poverty is not a problem in the USA – in fact, the material deprivation score is rather high compared with north-western Europe. But there is no support for the assertion that the poor do not, or no longer, benefit from favourable economic conditions. Contrary to the common narrative, Meyer and Sullivan's expenditure poverty data identify the high-growth periods – the late 1980s, and the 1990s after the 'Savings and Loans' crisis – as particularly beneficial to the poor. A discrepancy between income and expenditure, most pronounced at the bottom of the income spectrum, has also been observed in the case of Ireland (Madden, 2000: 197–8).

Spending poverty and income poverty data have not just evolved differently over the past, but also provide different present-day poverty profiles. In the UK, just over half of those in relative income poverty are in relative spending poverty. But risk profiles nevertheless differ. If income were replaced by spending, the group-specific poverty risk of the self-employed would almost halve. It would also fall, albeit from a high level, for those presently seeking work, and to a lesser extent for the unoccupied (Brewer et al., 2006a). The former is probably due to consumption smoothing, the latter to benefit under-reporting. Measured poverty would rise drastically for pensioners, whose recorded spending is, on average, lower than their recorded income. Individual motivations for a particular spending pattern are, of course, not recorded, so this could be read in a more optimistic or a more pessimistic way: the elderly may have a higher propensity to save, or they may be more insecure about their financial prospects.

Benefits in kind

Income-based poverty statistics record cash income – that is, market income and government cash transfers. They omit the value of publicly provided services that are offered free, or below market rates, at the point of use. Some of these services have a distributional impact, which is most obvious for benefits in kind. Social housing, social tariffs and free medical prescriptions are generally targeted at low-income groups via a means test, albeit not counted as part of income. But universally provided public services have a distributional effect as well. If people at all income levels use public services to the same extent, then adding the monetary value of their service consumption to individual incomes would elevate lower incomes relatively more. This makes income-based poverty measures sensitive to the structure of public spending. In a hypothetical welfare state in which *all* benefits are provided in kind the poor would have no money income, but access to free housing, free transport, free food, free medical care, free recreational facilities, etc.: an income-based measure would display grinding poverty. If the relative importance of in-kind and in-cash benefits differs across countries and/or changes over time, cross-country comparisons and/or time-series are affected.

Adding the cost of publicly provided services to individual incomes, using utilisation rates for such services, produces a more equal income distribution in all OECD countries (OECD, 2008: 224–45). For cross-country comparisons, the bias produced by the omission of services in kind does not seem to be a systematic one. Adding the cost of public education, healthcare and social housing to incomes reduces income inequalities, and the effect is generally more pronounced in the more unequal countries. But country rankings by inequality are largely unaffected. The familiar pattern is repeated with a somewhat narrower spread: the Scandinavians are still the most equal, continental Europe is in the middle, the English-speaking and the Mediterranean countries remain the most unequal.

But time-series comparisons may be more affected, as Browning (1989) shows for the USA. When the US poverty measure was devised, benefits in kind hardly existed: programmes such as Medicaid were just about to be created. By the mid-1980s, public benefits in kind had come to represent 70 per cent of US welfare spending (ibid.). Indeed, Browning points out that increasing the provision of free services can actually *raise* the poverty rate, by weakening incentives to earn the corresponding cash income. Using more up-to-date data, Wolff (2009) shows that when adding the cost of Medicaid, Medicare, food stamps and subsidised housing to income, the poverty rate can fall by up to five percentage points.

No similar evidence is available for the UK, but judging from the data provided by Sefton et al. (2009: 40–43), a similar picture emerges. The lowest-income groups contain a disproportionately large share of children and elderly people, leading to higher utilisation rates of health and education services. Public spending on these items has increased over time.

Unfortunately, adding the cost of in-kind services to incomes is a highly unsatisfactory approach, since the cost of these services tells us nothing about low-income groups' valuation of them. Sefton et al. believe that 'the amount of expenditure is a reasonable measure of its worth to recipients' (ibid.: 40). But these services are not offered and sold on markets, where consumers' valuations of them could be revealed. The entitlements are neither fungible, nor are there close substitutes available in the market, whose price could serve as an acceptable proxy. The method only shows that, for example, Medicaid, the federal health insurance for poor Americans, is expensive. It does not show that the American poor receive good healthcare. It shows that low-income groups in Britain have higher utilisation rates of healthcare and education services, but not that these services are especially 'pro-poor'. The middle classes may well be able to obtain better value from such government-provided services because sophisticated methods are necessary in order to improve provision in the case of dissatisfaction: for example, by moving home or articulating detailed complaints to a headteacher of a school. Evans (2008: 41–2) argues that the NHS has a pro-middle-class bias.

10 THE ROLE OF PRODUCT MARKETS AND PRICE DEVELOPMENTS

Below the price level aggregate

Differences in income or expenditure translate into differences in living standards – but not in a linear way: differences in living standards can widen or narrow drastically without any changes in incomes or expenditure. Concentrating on income and/or expenditure is like looking at one blade of a pair of scissors in isolation. It ignores changes in product markets, the pair of scissors' other blade: such changes affect different subgroups in different ways.

A representative consumption basket for poor households is not simply a miniature version of a representative consumption basket for middle-class households. The poor and the middle classes consume different things. Changes in the price of a given item will therefore affect different people in different ways, and changes in the structure of relative prices can alter both relative and absolute living standards. Relative prices are, of course, changing all the time. Table 16 shows some of the huge variations occurring below the surface of the Consumer Price Index (CPI) aggregate over a decade.

But conventional poverty measures, whether relative or absolute, do not account for these changes at all.

Table 16 **Change in various components of the Consumer Price Index (CPI) between 1999 and 2009**

	Change in CPI-component, UK, 1999–2009
Liquid fuels	+174%
Gas	+165%
Electricity	+83%
Transport services	+62%
Water supply	+52%
Food and non-alcoholic drinks	+33%
CPI, all items	+20%
Recreation and culture	–1%
Household appliances	–17%
Telephone equipment and services	–19%
Financial services	–23%
Clothing and footwear	–45%
Information-processing equipment	–88%

This problem can be illustrated by considering a stylised, hypothetical society with three social strata, the 'poor', the 'middle class' and the 'rich'. Each represents one third of the population. Expenditure levels are uniform within but differ across strata. The poor spend 140 gold coins per year, the middle class 300 and the rich 500 (Table 17a).

Table 17a **Three social groups in a hypothetical society and their expenditure levels**

Social group	Expenditure in gold coins
Poor	140
Middle class	300
Rich	500

Since the median expenditure is 300 gold coins, the poverty line, set at 50 per cent of the median, would be 150 gold coins. People in the bottom group fall below the poverty line.

There are three types of consumer goods: a basic, a convenience and a luxury good, with unit prices of 10, 20 and 30 gold coins respectively (Table 17b).

Table 17b **Three types of consumer goods in a hypothetical society and their unit costs**

Good	Unit price in gold coins
Basic (B)	10
Convenience (C)	20
Luxury (L)	30

Consumption patterns are uniform within but differ across strata. They are shown in Table 17c:

Table 17c **Consumption patterns in a hypothetical society**

Consumption breakdown (units of each good)	Cost
Poor	
10 basic	100
2 convenience	40
0 luxury	0
Total expenditure of the poor	140
Middle class	
14 basic	140
5 convenience	100
2 luxury	60
Total expenditure of the middle class	300
Rich	
16 basic	160

Consumption breakdown (units of each good)	Cost
8 convenience	160
6 luxury	180
Total expenditure of the rich	500

In the next year, the unit price of the basic good drops from 10 to 5 gold coins. This could be the result of a cut in import tariffs, the abolition of licences or other barriers to entry in the basic goods market, or increased use of economies of scale. Consumption patterns adjust in the following way:

Table 17d **Consumption patterns in the same society after a fall in the price of the basic good**

Consumption breakdown (units of each good)	Cost
Poor	
10 basic	50
3 convenience	60
1 luxury	30
Total expenditure of the poor	140
Middle class	
14 basic	70
7 convenience	140
3 luxury	90
Total expenditure of the middle class	300
Rich	
16 basic	80
9 convenience	180
8 luxury	240
Total expenditure of the rich	500

For the economy as a whole, the effect of the price fall is equivalent to an increase in real expenditure of 21 per cent, because the inflation rate[1] is −21 per cent and nominal expenditure is unchanged. Table 17d converts the price decrease into an equivalent increase in real expenditure, by expressing the cost of the new expenditure pattern in terms of the old prices. It shows that there is no impact on the distribution and thus on relative poverty. The poverty line also rises by 21 per cent in real terms, and remains above the expenditure of the poor (182 > 170).

Adjusting for the change in the aggregate price level, which is a mere average, however, does not take account of the fact that inflation affects the three groups in different ways. Since the poor dedicate a larger share of their budgets to the basic good than the other groups, the price drop has a larger impact on this group. Calculating group-specific inflation rates, based on each group's unique consumption pattern, shows that the poor actually experience an inflation rate of −36 per cent, compared with −23 per cent for the middle class and −16 per cent for the rich.[2]

When expressing each group's new equivalent expenditure by adjusting for the group-specific inflation rate, the expenditure of the poor rises above the poverty line (190 > 185). The fall in the price of B is now identified as a poverty-tackling factor while using the conventional method of measuring poverty it is not. This shows that relative indicators are unable to detect changes in the relative price structure with a pro-poor bias. The same goes

---

1   The inflation rate is calculated using the Paasche Index $\Sigma(pt+1 * qt+1) / \Sigma (pt * qt+1)$. The total cost of today's spending is compared with what it would have cost to purchase the same goods at yesterday's prices.

2   In this hypothetical case, unrealistically, there is no substitution effect, i.e. no individual responds to the fact that B has become cheaper relative to C and L by increasing consumption of B. In reality, it is reasonable to expect that substitution effects for many 'basic' consumption goods would be strongest among the low-income strata. This would strengthen the argument presented here further.

for quasi-absolute measures, where the poverty line is uprated by the general rate of inflation, and not by the price changes faced specifically by the poor.

Table 17e **The impact of the price change on real incomes**

Stratum/total cost	Income in period t (in gold coins)	Average inflation rate	Income in period t+1, expressed in period t-prices, adjusted by average inflation	Stratum-specific inflation rates	Income in period t+1, expressed in t-prices, adjusted by stratum-specific inflation
Poor	140	−21%	170	−36%	190
Middle class	300	−21%	364	−23%	370
Rich	500	−21%	606	−16%	580
Poverty line (half median income)	150		182		185

The policy conclusions are wide-ranging. Poverty measures that focus predominantly on nominal incomes will favour policies that also focus predominantly on nominal incomes. If, on the other hand, we pursue an anti-poverty strategy that leaves the level and distribution of nominal income/expenditure unchanged but which involves cutting trade barriers, reducing planning controls, decreasing legal barriers to market entry, easing regulatory supply-side restrictions and so on, this could be extremely effective, but the benefit would not tend to show in poverty statistics. If these policies lead to a tumbling of the cost of housing, food, clothing, energy and transport, the poor would gain in both relative and absolute terms. Yet as long as the nominal distribution of income is unchanged, relative poverty measures would detect no change at all, and quasi-absolute measures would capture only a small part of the effect.

Regional price differences

Being blind to price development in general, conventional poverty measures do not take account of regional differences in price levels either. In large countries with pronounced regional disparities such as the UK, this has implications for the geographical identification of poverty. Regional price indices for the UK are generally not available except for a single year, 2004/05. Using these data, Phillips (2008) adjusts incomes by regional price levels, and recalculates the conventional relative poverty rate of each region. It shows that this adjustment has a major impact on the poverty profile of the nation. Without adjustments for regional price differences, poverty is highest in the North-East of England, Northern Ireland, the West Midlands and Wales, while London occupies a middle rank. After the adjustment, the poverty rate is highest in London, rising by more than four percentage points. In Yorkshire, the North-East and Wales, the poverty rate drops by three percentage points or more.

Frugal innovation

In a number of consumer good industries, we frequently witness developments which make the everyday consumption experiences of poor people more similar to those of wealthier people, even as the distribution of incomes or expenditure is untouched. In some markets, this is achieved through an entrepreneurial strategy which has more recently been labelled 'frugal innovation', defined by *The Economist* as 'taking the needs of poor consumers as a starting point and working backwards. Instead of adding ever more bells and whistles, they [the frugal innovators] strip the products down to their bare essentials' (Economist, 2010a). Frugal innovation is by no means a new phenomenon, but merely a more sophisticated form of product differentiation. As product markets mature, they develop different market segments, tailored to the wallets of different consumer groups. They develop luxury versions, standard versions and bare-bones versions of the same core product. This process has the potential of making previously unattainable products available to the poor, albeit in cruder and simpler variants. It can be driven by technological or organisational innovations. Meyer and Sullivan (2007: 5) note that the US CPI suffers, among other shortcomings, from an 'outlet bias', which is 'the inadequate accounting for the movement of purchases toward low price discount or big box stores'.

The equalising effect of product market differentiation can be seen by comparing the European and the Latin American markets for short-haul flights. The Latin American market is comparatively poorly differentiated. Under these circumstances, buying or not buying a flight ticket is more often a *binary* choice: 'Being able to afford a flight' means 'being able to afford the fares of one or two particular companies'. When air travel is a yes-or-no decision, even small differences in income can translate into large differences in access to good air travel.

In the diversified European air travel market, the impact of income is a different one. In the European market, more money buys more on-board services, more legroom, more convenient flight hours, access to more conveniently located airports, more flexible booking policies, more gestures of goodwill, higher weight limits for luggage and many more convenient amenities. But it does not buy more of the core product, 'air travel'. The same logic applies to most consumer electronics, and to goods available in discounters. In differentiated product markets income differences become less important for access to core products than in markets in which purchasing decisions are closer to either-or decisions. As Wilkinson (2009: 6–7) put it: '[O]ver time, the everyday experience of consumption among the less fortunate has become in many ways more like that of their wealthier compatriots. This is a huge egalitarian triumph. A widescreen plasma television is a delight, but a cheap 19-inch TV is enough to allow a viewer to laugh at *Shrek*.'

A poverty indicator that reflects these developments could have implications for both anti-poverty policies directly and for the public debate more widely. The aims of having an equitable distribution of nominal incomes and of having highly developed, differentiated product markets may often be compatible with one another, but they can also be in conflict. If the development of differentiated product markets with 'pro-poor segments' is a policy aim, then the most obvious recommendations to achieve this aim would be free trade, open access to markets, absence of supply-side restrictions and unrestrained technological progress. But, paradoxically, the widely held view is that downward pressures on wages arising from trade with low-wage countries, alongside skill-biased technological progress, have sharply increased inequalities in the West. These perceptions are at the heart of the anti-globalisation movement and have long disseminated into the political mainstream. According to a global poll by the BBC World Service (2008), the majority of the population in nearly all major developed countries is convinced that globalisation is advancing 'too fast' and that its benefits and burdens are not 'distributed fairly'. The UK is no outlier.

Caritas Europa (2010) captures these popular sentiments:

> Globalisation and technological progress lead to increased global competition in the labour market. Flexibility, wage reductions, irregular working hours and the constant need for additional training exert a pressure that many people can no longer withstand. The number of working individuals who earn too little – known as the 'working poor' – is increasing in all European countries. These reports are chastening. Is the whole of Europe growing poor? On the other hand, every day in the street or at school we see people wearing the latest fashions, talking on the latest mobile phone.

Clearly, those who share these concerns – whether they are founded or not is a separate debate – are looking only at one side of the equation, which is the distribution of *nominal* incomes. Both the global division of labour and technological advancement are also associated with the emergence of low-cost substitutes for previously expensive products. Even if they did lead to a widening of the distribution of nominal incomes, they would also have an effect to the contrary, through what Wilkinson (2009: 7) labels the 'compression in the range of material experience'.

A poverty indicator that captures this compression, even if only very imperfectly, would shed a different light on many contemporary debates. Contrary to presently used indicators, it would evaluate developments such as trade integration and technological progress not only by their impact on the range of nominal incomes, but also by their impact on the 'range of material experiences'. It would recognise the pro-poor bias of competition and productivity growth, consumer choice, diversification and the emergence of low-cost market segments.

11 TOWARDS AN EXPENDITURE-BASED 'CONSENSUAL BUDGET STANDARD APPROACH'

Poverty in the UK is still a major public concern and it is likely to remain so in the foreseeable future. In the 2010 election, the issue featured in all major parties' manifestoes (Labour Party, 2010: 63–5; Conservative Party, 2010: 15, 37; Liberal Democrats, 2010: 50). Various influential publications have been written about domestic poverty (see Stewart et al., 2009; Horton and Gregory, 2009) and a whole landscape of advocacy groups, charities and NGOs deal with the topic or particular aspects of it. Given the topic's prominence, it is surprising how little we know about domestic poverty more than a century after Booth and Rowntree. The conventional poverty measures are all beset with grave flaws. They can easily convey systematically wrong impressions about poverty, and encourage flawed policy recommendations.

The problems of relative measures summarised

Relative poverty measures are a meaningless construct. They gained prominence because they were seen to be rooted in their social context, reflecting the cost of participating in a specific society in a specific time. As Townsend (1980) put it, 'a relative measure's greatest theoretical virtue is that it is entirely grounded in national and historical context'. But they failed to live up to this purpose. Far from reflecting anything about time-specific and place-specific social norms, they simply tie the poverty line to a statistical average, which need not have any social relevance. Far from factoring in the cost of complying with social norms, they treat increases in median incomes as a burden on the poor. They convey the dubious impression that the least well off derive no benefit from improvements in their material living conditions as such. It is undeniable that common perceptions about what is considered an adequate living standard are not formed in a vacuum. But this does not mean that the value of more spacious housing, healthier food, greater mobility, greater access to cultural and educational activities, or to goods and services related to health and wellbeing, is nullified when others enjoy them too.

At the same time, relative measures fail to register developments that do affect the least well off in very tangible ways. The emergence of relative measures began with a sound critique of Rowntree's Budget Standard Approach. This approach was criticised for being based on a hypothetical basket of necessities which had little to do with what poor people actually bought. It was therefore seen as socially irrelevant. But, ironically, Rowntree's approach had at least some overlap with people's actual consumption habits, while relative standards are completely divorced from them. Relative standards contain no information about what it is that poor people can or cannot afford. Based exclusively on the distribution of nominal incomes, they are completely blind to developments in product markets which affect the living standards of the least well off.

Quasi-absolute measures are little improvement

Nevertheless, replacing an income-based relative measure with an expenditure-based quasi-absolute measure also leaves a host of poverty measurement problems unsolved. First of all, a quasi-absolute poverty rate has no meaningful interpretation. A poverty line should correspond to a living standard which can, by some theoretical criterion, be interpreted as a decent minimum standard for a particular society at a particular time. If the sole purpose of this measure is to check how the living standards of the least well off have evolved in absolute terms, then one might as well simply focus on the evolution of real income or real expenditure of the bottom deciles or percentiles. There is no reason to benchmark them against some randomly chosen yardstick which has no meaning of its own. Even if a quasi-absolute poverty measure reflected the social norms and expectations of a particular time and place, and therefore did have a clear and meaningful interpretation, it would not *remain* meaningful for a long time. Social norms and expectations change. Poverty is a lack of the means necessary for healthy physical sustenance. But it is also a lack of the means necessary to comply with social norms, participate in context-specific social activities, and to attain what is widely considered a 'decent minimum standard'.

In the UK, large-scale surveys show that between 80 and 100 per cent of the population consider a damp-free, heated home with an indoor bathroom, an indoor toilet, a bed for every family member and a refrigerator to be necessities, as opposed to desirable amenities (Gordon et al., 2000: 43–5). No long-time-series or cross-country comparisons are available for surveys of this type. But surely, these perceptions would have been different in the UK two generations earlier, and they are likely to be very different in many middle-income countries today.

It is also noteworthy that a majority considers celebrations on special occasions, presents for friends, the ability to afford some (unspecified) leisure activity and some out-of-school activity for children necessities. This highlights, again, that poverty is about social participation as much as it is about physical sustenance, and that it is a context-specific phenomenon which changes over time. A fixed poverty line becomes obsolete eventually. The US poverty line, which has been in use since the mid-1960s, does not demonstrate the opposite. Meyer and Sullivan (2007: 15) show that owing to an upward bias in the measurement of inflation, 'in practice, our official poverty standard is a partly relative one, incorporating about one percent real growth per year'.

Quasi-absolute poverty standards also share one major weakness with relative ones: they are blind to product market developments which affect the living standards of the less well off. Fixed poverty lines are updated by the rate of inflation, which is the wrong tool. It measures changes in the cost of a basket of goods which resembles the consumption pattern of average households, not of poor households. This makes quasi-absolute measures just as unable as relative ones to allow for the role of trade, competition and innovation in the alleviation of poverty.

The relative advantage of material deprivation measures

Of the poverty measures currently in use, it is the material deprivation measure which best fulfils the criteria outlined here. Based on a tangible basket of goods and services, this measure has a clear and meaningful interpretation. A person's material deprivation poverty status depends on the number of items in the basket that they cannot afford, not on how they compare with some arbitrary benchmark. Nonsensical outcomes such as falling poverty rates amid falling living standards do not occur with this measure. To some extent, material deprivation standards are even able to capture product market developments and changes in access to benefits in kind. Other things being equal, changes in the market prices of the items in the basket will affect people's ability to afford them, and hence the material deprivation score. Also, increases (decreases) in the generosity of benefits in kind will free (bind) resources for the purchase of other things, which will affect the material deprivation score. Misreporting of some income sources, or short-term fluctuations, is also not an issue. What determines the material deprivation score is *whether* a household can afford the items in the basket, not *how* they manage to achieve this.

Shortcomings of material deprivation measures

But material deprivation has its shortcomings nonetheless. First of all, the basket of necessities is assembled in an arbitrary way. There is no guarantee that the items in the basket resonate with what a majority of the population, or what most poor people themselves, would consider 'necessities'. The basket need not coincide with common perceptions of what represents a decent minimum standard. Therefore, strictly speaking, material deprivation indicators measure low consumption standards, but do not actually measure poverty.

Second, material deprivation measures cannot distinguish between material constraints and preferences. It has been shown that respondents who lack 'necessities' on a material deprivation list sometimes possess 'luxuries' (McKay, 2004; Myck, 2005). When survey participants lack an item, they are asked whether this was because they cannot afford the item or because they do not want it, but this does not separate preferences from constraints at all. The reason for the mismatch is neither misreporting nor 'wasteful' spending, but heterogeneity of preferences. These households really are unable to afford some of the items on the list – but only because they have already bought other items that are not on the list. They are not being asked whether they could have afforded the item if they had relinquished other things. This means that material deprivation levels will be systematically inflated, which would explain why material deprivation still occurs among high-income groups.

Material deprivation is a direct measure of living standards, unrelated to income or expenditure. This enables the measure to capture unobserved variables that affect living standards, but it also makes it reliant on household's self-classification, with no recourse to objective data.

Material deprivation is also the most rough-and-ready approach among poverty measures, because many of the items in the basket are specified at a considerable level of generality. A 'holiday away from home' could be anything from a week in a spa resort at Lake Geneva to a week in a bed-and-breakfast in Blackpool. The items on a material deprivation list may well mean different things to different people, which will invariably affect their answers.

Material deprivation is a back-of-the-envelope indicator of a low consumption standard and not an accurate indicator of poverty. While this means that the level of material deprivation is not very informative, however, its trend and variation across population subgroups might very well be. Material deprivation may still be able to help us find sensible policy recommendations.

Consensual material deprivation

Poverty is a highly abstract concept, especially when understood as impeded social participation, which means different things to different people. There will never be a consensus on what precisely constitutes poverty. But this does not make poverty measurement completely futile. Poverty is not merely in the eye of the beholder. There is, in fact, a fairly robust consensus in society on what constitutes necessities. This can be seen in the results of large-scale surveys such as the British Poverty and Social Exclusion Survey (PSE). In the PSE, respondents are presented with a large list of goods and services, and are asked to identify which of them they consider necessities that everybody should have, and which of them they merely consider desirable. An item qualifies as a necessity when the majority of respondents consider it so (see Gordon et al., 2000; Patanzis et al., 2006). This approach is known as 'Consensual Material Deprivation' (CMD); it leads to a material deprivation index where the basket of necessities is not chosen by researchers, but by the survey respondents' majoritarian decision. The outcome contains a surprise: people may disagree widely when asked about the definition of poverty in abstract terms, but there is a large degree of agreement in the identification of tangible necessities. As the authors of the PSE survey emphasise, there is nothing close to a perfect consensus. But the important insight is that for those items which a large majority considers necessities, deviations from this majority view are random ones: with some exceptions, responses do not differ systematically across social subgroups: 'otherwise, the definition of a necessity would just become the opinion of one group against another' (Patanzis et al., 2006: 114).

This subgroup neutrality, albeit not without exceptions,

stands in stark contrast to relative definitions. Median incomes and hence relative poverty lines differ vastly across regions and subgroups. England and Scotland differ in median incomes, so their relative poverty rates would be vastly different if they were treated as nations in their own right. But when asked to assemble a basket of necessities, English and Scottish respondents would, by and large, include the same items. With a consensual material deprivation poverty measure, a secession of Scotland from the UK would be relatively unimportant for the English and Scottish poverty rates.

The PSE survey is available for three different years: 1983, 1990 and 1999.[1] Extrapolating from these three snapshots, the general tendency is that people's understanding of what constitutes a necessity becomes more encompassing over time, but in a gradual way. The 1999 basket contains a number of items which the 1983 basket did not yet contain: the telephone entered, as did an outfit for social occasions, inviting friends and children's friends for a meal or a snack at regular intervals, and a few other items. In practice, this gives the consensual material deprivation standard a superficial similarity to a relative poverty line that follows median incomes with an elasticity of less than one. But its underlying logic is a very different one. The implicit consensual material deprivation poverty line does not mechanically follow median incomes or

1   The 1999 CMD basket includes (merging similar items): beds/bedding, heating, damp-free home, home decoration, replace/repair electrical goods and furniture, two meals a day, fresh fruit and vegetables daily, meat/fish/equivalent every other day, roast joint/equivalent once a week, refrigerator, freezer, washing machine, telephone, TV, contents insurance, warm/waterproof coat, appropriate clothing, all-weather shoes, access to transport, celebrating/attending special occasions, leisure activity, inviting friends and family for a meal, presents for friends and family, annual holiday, dictionary, medicines, regular savings.

any other variable. Its increase over time is not a result of rising average incomes per se, but only insofar as rising average incomes have changed social interactions and thus raised social participation costs. The telephone has become a necessity because it is a 'network good' – it becomes more valuable (and eventually indispensable) as more people acquire it: it might be difficult to obtain a job or keep an eye on vulnerable relatives, for example, without access to a telephone. This is a social change which could conceivably have occurred with stagnant median incomes as well – just as rising median incomes could have been channelled into the acquisition of goods and services that do not affect social norms, or only to a minor extent (such as foreign holidays). The approval rating of some items on the list has remained unchanged or even fallen, despite higher median incomes and higher prevalence rates of the items.

No equivalent which is nearly as encompassing as the PSE exists on the EU level. Guio et al. (2009), however, provide a basic version of a consensual material deprivation measure for the EU-27, which suggests that large overlaps in the consensual identification of necessities exist even across the EU. The common denominator is probably not large enough to justify the use of a pan-European poverty line for the EU-27. There are items such as computers, which are considered necessities in some European countries but not in others (indeed, they may be more necessary in some poorer countries than some richer countries, depending on the extent to which, for example, broadband infrastructure has been rolled out). But, even so, these differences are not nearly as large as the differences between national relative poverty lines. If poverty in the EU was measured by national consensual material deprivation standards, implicit poverty lines would, again, superficially resemble weakly relative poverty lines. They would probably be higher in wealthier countries than in poorer ones – but not to such an extent as to cancel out the large differences in the absolute living standards of the least well off. By and large, the subgroup neutrality holds at the EU level as well, albeit, unsurprisingly, with exceptions and with noise.

Beyond a consensual material deprivation measure: towards a new measure of poverty

So, if there is a reliable minimum consensus in society on the identification of necessities, then this should be the basis of a poverty measure. But the poverty measure should not be the consensual material deprivation measure itself, which suffers from the same problems as conventional material deprivation measures. Such measures are very imprecise because they do not make use of objective data such as income or expenditure. They cannot distinguish between households that forgo basic goods because of genuine deprivation and households that forgo them because they prioritise different things. This is why material deprivation measures often classify people who lack basic goods, but who simultaneously possess 'luxuries', as 'deprived'. This bias can be expected to be particularly strong in economies with highly differentiated product markets.

The consensual material deprivation measure is useful in identifying a majoritarian basket of necessities which is genuinely rooted in its social context, but not for checking whether a given individual is actually poor or not. This makes it, as it were, the mirror-inverted reflection of Seebohm Rowntree's long-abandoned Budget Standard Approach. This approach, based on actual market prices and actual household income, was a very accurate measure of whether a given household could attain a predefined consumption pattern. A Budget Standard Approach can capture relevant price developments and local differences in price levels like no other poverty measure. But its basic flaw, which led to its eventual abandonment, was that this predefined consumption pattern itself was not socially relevant. So if the respective strengths of Budget Standard Approach and consensual material deprivation are complementary, why not combine the two measures into an integrated 'Consensual Material Deprivation/Budget Standard Approach' (CBSA), and measure poverty in this way?

The CBSA would work like this. In a large-scale survey similar to the PSE, people would select a basket of necessities by majority decision (or some other form of consensus). As soon as the list of necessities is assembled, it should be converted into a consumption basket. This is the bridge from the consensual material deprivation part to the Budget Standard Approach part of the indicator. In research of a more qualitative type, there have already been experiments with CBSAs: the Joseph Rowntree Foundation's (2010) 'Minimum Income Standard' is the cost of necessity baskets established through interviews with smaller focus groups. There is no reason why the approach should not work on a large scale. The broad item categories identified in the consensual material deprivation survey should be translated into tangible products that are really being bought and sold. The guideline for this translation should be revealed preferences, as documented in national expenditure surveys. By taking account of revealed preferences, the CBSA would contain an additional layer of information, which is not present in consensual material deprivation measures. This would anchor the CBSA more firmly in its social context.

In the British case, the relevant data source to identify revealed preferences is the Living Cost and Food Survey (LCF). For example, if a washing machine enters the list of necessities, then some low-cost washing machine which really is frequently bought by people on low incomes should enter the basket, not the average price of a washing machine. The market prices of the items in the basket, if possible collected at the local level to account for geographical price variations, should then be added up to a poverty line. The price of goods that are provided free at the point of use, such as benefits in kind, would be set to zero. This means that the poverty line of a country where, for example, dental treatment is covered by the statutory health system would be lower than the poverty line of an otherwise identical country in which it was not provided. For volatile expenses such as the cost of medical treatments or repairs, the price of a standard insurance policy should enter where available. For other irregular expenses, a long-term average would enter. For the technical issues, an appropriate guideline would be the highly sophisticated 'Market-Based Measure' assembled by Statistics Canada, one of the few Budget Standard Approach poverty measures still in use (Hatfield, 2002; Michaud et al., 2004).

The poverty line, or the separate poverty lines for various household types, would then be the yardstick against which household expenditure is benchmarked. Households would be classified as poor if their total expenditure was below the poverty line, because these are the households that could not afford the whole basket if they wanted it. Unlike with a consensual material deprivation measure, poverty status would be unaffected by actual purchasing decisions.

Households whose expenditure is above the poverty line, but which nevertheless forgo some items of the basket because they choose to buy different things, are not classified as poor. They could have afforded the whole basket but chose not to do so. A consensual material deprivation measure cannot take account of either possibility; a CBSA can. This is important because the existence of a minimum consensus on what constitutes necessities does not imply that everybody has the same views or will make the same purchasing decisions. It only means that when a majority classifies an item as a necessity, deviations from this majority view are unlikely to be systematically related to socio-demographic characteristics. But deviations will, of course, occur. Also, there is no reason why there should be a perfect overlap between what people consider necessary in principle, and what they really do buy. Rowntree's mistake of building a benchmark around a hypothetical puritan consumption pattern, and then wondering why nobody adheres to it, must not be repeated. This is why the basket should be 'consensually' determined, and why there should be no exclusion of items on paternalistic grounds (as the PSE survey does for cigarettes). But we should not make the opposite mistake, as the consensual material deprivation measure effectively does, by treating people as deprived whenever they do not spend their money on whatever the consensus agrees it should be spent on.

12 ADVANTAGES OF THE NEW POVERTY MEASURE

While not without faults of its own, the CBSA could avoid many of the shortfalls of conventional poverty measures. Relative indicators change whenever the imputed reference group is changed. This would not be the case for the CBSA. Whether the list of necessities is decided on by consensus of the citizens of Greater London, of England, of the UK, or of north-western Europe is unlikely to make a large difference. Only if societies at very different stages of economic development were amalgamated into a single poverty assessment domain would the approach cease to be applicable. Insofar as the consensus regarding the relevant basket was different in different areas or countries, this would lead to a perfectly appropriate difference in the poverty standard.

Relative indicators profess to measure the cost of complying with social norms when what they really do is measure inequality. The CBSA depends more on the composition of common spending patterns, not so much on their aggregate level. In a society where telephones constitute a rare luxury, it is possible to be fully integrated into society without possessing one. If telephone ownership becomes near-universal, the item becomes a necessity. The spread of telephone ownership therefore entails a rise in the cost of social participation. There are many goods to which this logic could not be applied to a comparable extent, however, even if ownership rates are high. It would be difficult to argue that electric tin openers are necessary for social participation, even where nearly everybody owns one. A consensual list of necessities is fine-grained enough to differentiate between goods which change social interactions and goods which do not.

This measure would also manage to factor time into account. Items enter the list of necessities as soon as they have acquired the status of being a necessity in the view of the consensus. It is not enough for the item to be affordable for median income earners.

Relative measures frequently show falling poverty rates during recessions. With a CBSA, this would not happen because the list of necessities is highly unlikely to adjust downwards again in the short term (it might adjust downwards, however, in a period of a prolonged decline in living standards). Similarly, in a period of rapid economic growth, the poverty measure is likely to fall under this approach when it might rise under a relative measure.

The CBSA would also respond directly to changes in the structure of relative prices which are unfavourable for low earners. Other things being equal, rising costs of goods such as housing, energy or food would raise the poverty line. If low-cost substitutes for items in the basket emerge, the former can replace the latter and, other things being equal, the poverty line would fall. If prices are assembled at a decentralised level, as in the Canadian 'Market-Based Measure' (MBM), regional variations in price levels would be reflected as well. The poverty line for London would certainly be substantially higher than its Welsh or Scottish equivalent.

A CBSA would also differ sharply from conventional absolute poverty indices. The poverty rate would have a clear and meaningful interpretation. The poverty line would not be fixed, but slowly rising over time, responding to social changes. It would be tied to the cost of the goods and services that poor people really purchase, not to economic aggregates such as the general price level.

This approach is not presently applied in the UK, so it cannot be known how CBSA poverty evolved in recent years. But the most likely answer is that the last decade has not been a glorious one as far as poverty mitigation is concerned, not just because of the economic downturn. In 1999, total weekly expenditure of households in the lowest and the second-lowest deciles amounted to £120 and £147 respectively (Office for National Statistics, 2000: 14). By 2008, it had increased to £154 and £200 in nominal terms (Office for National Statistics, 2010a: 35). Adjusted by the CPI, this would correspond to a modest improvement. But what the CPI conceals is that price increases were skewed against the poor (Institute for Fiscal Studies, 2008, 2009). On balance, this points to a lost decade for poverty mitigation. It is possible that we have been focusing on the wrong policies – providing enhancements to income rather than focusing on repealing those government policies that might raise the price of certain goods (such as the Common Agricultural Policy, 'green' energy policies, planning constraints and so on).

PART III: POVERTY MEASUREMENT AND GOVERNMENT POLICY

'[R]eal income growth can have an impact in the short term, but over the long haul the only way to reduce poverty is to bring people closer to average living standards.'

Callan et al. (1998)

'The solution lies not in the division, but in the multiplication of the social product.'

Ludwig Erhard (1956)

13 POVERTY MEASUREMENT IN THE UK

Over the last decade, poverty measures have demonstrably shaped anti-poverty policies – especially child poverty policies; these will be a focus of this chapter. Initially, there was a single target measure for child poverty. Additional ones have been added subsequently, supposedly to provide a more complete poverty profile. But these measures do not, as is often claimed, complement each other. If relative poverty rises, absolute poverty falls, and material deprivation stagnates (as happened in the UK for several years), then how does this combine into a coherent message? It would have been more sensible to address the shortcomings of the initial target measure, instead of adding further ones.

This chapter will evaluate the measures underlying the different child poverty targets, and other frequently cited measures. It will then show how they have influenced, and sometimes misled, social policies, and present alternative policies that are more compatible with a realistic poverty measure.

Relative child poverty target

The original target envisaged eliminating relative child poverty by 2020. This has now been revised to reducing relative poverty to 'less than ten per cent' (HM Treasury, Department for Children,

Schools and Families & Department for Work and Pensions, 2010: 10). The measure behind this target is meaningless in the ways described in the above chapters. It contains no information whatsoever about the ability of low-income families with children to afford sizeable living space, healthy food, learning materials, vacations, transport, or any other goods and services affecting child wellbeing. It is fully conceivable for the UK to experience a decade of Japan-style stagnation, accompanied by falling living standards for low-earning families, and still reach the child poverty target. It is equally possible to record steady improvements in low-earner families' access to all the amenities mentioned above, and still miss the target by a wide margin. The measure does not even capture the relative position of low-income families. It could show marked relative improvements amid a surge in the cost of essential goods such as housing or energy, if only the distribution of nominal income is compressed. A decline in self-employment, and other forms of employment with volatile remuneration, could also contribute to reaching the target amid declining living standards.

The measure should be abolished altogether. Inequality in the bottom half of the distribution is already well measured by the P50/P10 ratio, a common alternative (or complement) to the Gini-coefficient, even though it would be more sensible to apply this measure to expenditure data instead of income data.

'Deep poverty'

This is also a relative poverty measure which sets the threshold at 40 per cent of median income instead of the conventional 60 per cent. It was repeatedly used by representatives of the Conservative

Party as a supposedly more 'targeted' measure, to identify those most in need (Conservative Party, 2008; Hunt and Clark, 2007). All the shortfalls of the conventional relative measure apply to this one no less, since the criticisms do not depend on where precisely the threshold is set. But, at least in the UK context, 'deep poverty' is actually a worse measure than conventional relative poverty. Those with the very lowest incomes do not experience the lowest living standards, and this mismatch is most pronounced for the bottom few percentiles of the income distribution. A lower threshold produces a poverty population in which misclassified people represent a larger share. Also, those with the lowest living standards are located in an income range between 30 and 50 per cent of the median, so that the conventional relative poverty measure *accidentally* includes the genuinely poor, whereas the Conservative Party's measure excludes many of them, while over-emphasising those who merely experience temporary income fluctuations. The measure should be dropped.

Quasi-absolute child poverty target

The quasi-absolute child poverty target relies on a measure with a poverty line that is fixed in real terms – presently at 60 per cent of the real median income in 1998/99. This will later be adjusted to 60 per cent of the real median income in 2010/11. The Child Poverty Bill seeks to reduce its rate to less than 5 per cent by 2020 (HM Treasury, Department for Children, Schools and Families & Department for Work and Pensions, 2010: 11).

The advantage of this measure is that it avoids the anti-growth bias of relative measures. By and large, it records improvements when the real incomes of those who are least well off improve.

Over time, it will become more and more similar to 'deep poverty', because the poverty line will fall relative to contemporary median incomes. It will therefore increasingly suffer from the same problems as 'deep poverty'. The fact that it identifies those with the lowest reported incomes, not those with the lowest living standards, could be remedied by replacing reported income with expenditure.

But such a change would still not make this absolute measure a good measure of poverty. First, it would still largely ignore important changes in product markets and the relative price structure of consumer goods: it could indeed record falling poverty while living standards of the least well off are falling. Second, the measure has no meaningful interpretation. A poverty line should correspond to some minimum living standard determined in such a way that there is a reason for labelling those who do not reach this standard 'poor', and those who exceed it 'not poor'. A threshold of 60 per cent of the UK real median income of 1998 or 2010 does not fulfil this criterion. The measure is not particularly suitable for informing the public debate either. An interested lay observer is unlikely to have a clear idea about what kind of living standard corresponds to the poverty line.

For medium-term comparisons over time, the quasi-absolute measure is not uninformative. But it would be equally informative just to look at how real expenditure of parents at, say, the 5th or the 10th percentile of the expenditure distribution has developed over the same period, so the latter could just as well replace the quasi-absolute measure.

Persistent poverty target

More recently, a fourth measure has been added to the set of child poverty targets, namely a measure of 'persistent low income' or persistent relative poverty. It is defined as the proportion of households that fall below the contemporary relative poverty line in three out of four years. This measure may come closer to identifying the genuinely poor than the snapshot measures because it automatically filters out those who experience transitory low income. It is still highly imperfect because the focus should not be the duration of low-income spells per se, but whether households are able to bridge low-income spells through consumption smoothing or not. Depending on their prior earnings and savings record, some households may be able to withstand even a three-year-long low-income spell without sinking into material hardship, while others may sink into hardship with only a minimal time lag after the income reduction. From this perspective, instead of creating yet another poverty index made up of existing indices, it would have been more sensible to replace income with spending as a proxy for living standards. Also, the measure has no sensible interpretation, as far as poverty is concerned. If 60 per cent of contemporary median income is not a sensible benchmark measure for a single-year period, it is no more sensible over longer periods. All the other criticisms, such as blindness to developments in product markets, apply to persistent low income as well.

Like quasi-absolute poverty, for comparisons over a short or intermediate period of time, this measure is not uninformative. But it should be replaced by looking at real expenditure at the bottom of the distribution.

Combined material deprivation and low income poverty target

A further child poverty target counts the number of children living in households classified to be in material deprivation while also recording an income of less than 70 per cent of the median. Poverty by this measure fell by a quarter, from 20.8 to 15.6 per cent, between 1998 and 2006, and rose again to 17.1 per cent in 2008. This child poverty target is the most sensible of the government's targets. It has a meaningful interpretation; it is not tied to a benchmark of questionable relevance such as present or past median income. The measure also avoids nonsensical findings, such as identifying the self-employed as a high-risk group, and it does not decrease during recessions. It is the only one among the government's targets which captures regional variations in the cost of living:

> Holding other factors constant, including work and family status, it is estimated that, of all the regions, London has the lowest level of income-based poverty: all other regions are estimated to have much higher levels of income-based poverty. However, when we look at material-deprivation-based poverty, we see that London moves to have one of the highest levels of poverty and that the lowest levels can be found in Wales, Northern Ireland and Scotland. (Brewer et al., 2008a: 74)

Income-based relative poverty measures do not find these results. Like other material deprivation measures, however, this measure cannot separate preferences for not consuming particular items from constraints – or an inability to consume those items. An impression of this can be obtained by looking at the specific deprivations people report, because they include results that simply do not make sense. Almost a third of respondents with children profess that they could not afford to invite their children's friends for tea or a snack once a fortnight: an activity which costs next to nothing. For a much costlier activity, namely a family holiday of at least one week, the same rate is recorded (ibid.: 62). A third of the recorded materially deprived earn incomes above 70 per cent of the median, with deprivation being recorded even in high-income strata. In the combined material deprivation/low income measure, this is dealt with by simply chopping off the high-income deprived from the poverty count. This does, of course, not address the theoretical flaws that give rise to this counter-intuitive result in the first place. The basket of essentials is also assembled in a rather arbitrary way so that the measure may gauge low living standards but does not necessarily measure 'poverty'.

Nevertheless, among the child poverty targets, the material deprivation/low income measure is the closest relative of the Consensual Budget Standard Approach measure proposed above. The two would surely exhibit a sizeable correlation in terms of time trends, geographical variation and socio-economic risk factors.

Severe child poverty

'Severe child poverty' is an indicator used by the charity Save the Children (2010). It is essentially a more stringent version of the material deprivation/low income measure, with additional requirements for the material deprivation score and a lower income cut-off point (50 per cent of the median instead of 70 per cent). Like the material deprivation/low income measure, it is intuitively sensible, albeit prone to the above-mentioned short-comings of material deprivation.

So what do we know about child poverty?

Very few findings about child poverty are robust across different poverty indicators, so it is worth pointing out the few which are.

It is fairly clear that child poverty is indeed a long-term problem in the UK, and it is also clear that long-term detachment from the labour market plays an important role in explaining child poverty (albeit the magnitude of this latter point differs substantially across indicators). The often quoted 'one in three children' in child poverty is hyperbolic, and the comparison of relative rates between the UK, Poland and Hungary (e.g. UNICEF Innocenti Research Center, 2005 and 2007) is misleading. But the UK also fares poorly on various quasi-absolute and material deprivation measures of child poverty, both in cross-country and in time-series comparisons (see Table 18). In short, it is more than appropriate that the topic has received increased attention since the late 1990s.

The idea that weak labour market attachment should be a major problem in the UK would surely seem surprising to an outside observer. The UK labour market has performed strongly during most of the last two decades, especially in comparison with some of the Continental economies with their chronically high levels of unemployment. Despite being hit somewhat earlier by the crisis, the UK's unemployment rate in 2008 was still 1.4 percentage points below the average of the EU-27 using harmonised measures (Eurostat, 2009b: 38). It is well known that this partially reflects the large share of incapacity benefit

Table 18 **Child poverty in the UK, various measures**

	Quasi-absolute child poverty in 2000: PPP-converted US poverty line
UK	12.4%
US	8.7%
Germany	7.6%
Canada	6.9%
Austria	5.2%
	Quasi-absolute child poverty AHC: poverty line = 40% of 1998 median
UK 1970–79	13.1%
UK 1980–89	14.3%
UK 1990–99	13.5%
	Combined material deprivation + income < 70% of median
UK 1998/99	20.8%
UK 2004/05	17.1%
UK 2006/07	15.6%
UK 2008/09	17.1%
	'Severe child poverty' (= combined material deprivation + income < 50%)
UK 2004/05	11%
UK 2007/08	13%

Sources: Statistics from Smeeding (2006: 77); Institute for Fiscal Studies (2010); Office for National Statistics & Department for Work and Pensions (2009a: 76); Save the Children (2010); Joyce et al. (2010)

recipients, who do not appear in unemployment statistics. Even in terms of total employment rates, however, the UK ranked well above average (ibid.: 20). But the devil lurks below the surface of aggregates. The UK has a fairly low overall rate of economic inactivity – but it has a cross-household distribution of inactivity which makes it differ from other countries: the UK has an above-average share of economically inactive households, and above all, it has the EU-27's highest share of children living in households with no single member in gainful employment – 1.8 million children live in households where nobody works. As the New Policy Institute (New Policy Institute & Joseph Rowntree Foundation, 2007: 52) emphasises:

> Despite the falls in the number of children in workless households, the UK still has the highest proportion of its children living in workless households in any European Union country, its 16 per cent rate (in 2006) exceeding that of the next worst three (Bulgaria, Belgium and Hungary) by at least 2 percentage points and being around two-thirds higher than the rates in both France and Germany.

These comparators are well chosen, because they highlight the exceptionality of the UK's position. France and Germany have much higher overall rates of unemployment and economic inactivity, while Bulgaria and Hungary have high levels of unregistered, informal employment, which suggests that the UK effectively leads this country ranking by an even wider margin. Economic inactivity is not more prevalent in the UK than elsewhere, but it is unusually concentrated, and it affects children more than proportionally. Other countries have their own problems – not necessarily shared by the UK to the same degree – such as unemployment among young single people or older people; the UK, however, has a particular problem with workless households.

Nowhere in the employment statistics is the gap between the UK and the rest of the EU-27 larger than in the employment rate of single parents. Their group-specific employment rate of 55.5 per cent is seventeen percentage points below the western European average, and eight percentage points below the second-lowest rate in Poland. This is particularly significant because one in four children in the UK live in single-parent households, one of the highest proportions in the developed world (European Commission, 2009: 51). Accordingly, of the 1.8 million children living in workless households, 1.2 million live with a single parent. In other countries, single parenthood is either much less prevalent, or the vast majority of single parents are employed (see Table 19).

Table 19 **Prevalence of single parenthood versus employment situation of single parents**

	Proportion of children living in single-parent families < 10%	*Proportion of children living in single-parent families > 15%*
Employment rate of single parents < 70%	Netherlands Poland	UK
Employment rate of single parents > 80%		Sweden Denmark

Sources: Statistics from Eurostat (2009a: 48), HM Treasury, Department for Children, Schools and Families & Department for Work and Pensions (2010: 23) and European Commission (2009: 51)

Clearly, the absence of two adults in a household makes it more difficult for a parent to be in work, but it is striking that, in the UK, we not only have a low proportion of children in two-adult households but a low proportion of single parents in work.

These data suggest that our anti-poverty policies should be more subtle than the provision of income transfers. Policies that encourage a higher level of employment and, possibly, policies that do not discourage family formation may be more important.

Furthermore, the UK's state-dominated schooling system may lead to reduced human capital for the less well off and thus reduce their employment opportunities and the attractiveness of employment as compared with benefits and single parenthood. Though we do not cover all aspects of these policy issues here, if the UK is going to reduce poverty (especially as measured by some form of consensual material deprivation), then the focus should perhaps be on employment, economic growth, education and the way in which the welfare system discourages family formation.

14 CHILD POVERTY POLICIES

Employment or redistribution?

The adoption of the child poverty targets was followed by the adoption of a series of welfare reforms with two main objectives: making the tax-and-benefit system more redistributive towards low-income families with children, and promoting employment among them. Since redistributive policies generally weaken work incentives, these two goals are not easily reconcilable, and the poverty targets adopted were hardly an unbiased mediator between these conflicting goals. Building up earnings capacities is a lengthier process that will not have a strong impact on income-based poverty measures for a while. Nor is there a guarantee that low earnings will rise at the same pace as median incomes. The easiest way to get closer to an income-based, relative poverty target is to increase income transfers, targeted towards those with the lowest incomes, and to maximise take-up rates by not attaching any strings. This narrows the distance between the bottom and the middle of the income distribution directly and immediately. Whether employment increases is then comparatively unimportant in terms of meeting the poverty target. Adam et al. (2006: 19–21) look at summary measures of labour market incentives in the UK over time, and plot them against measures of relative poverty. They find that 'the [relative] poverty and inequality measures are highly correlated with all of the work incentive measures: average work incentives have tended to be strongest in years when poverty and inequality have been highest. These correlations range from −0.51 ... to −0.89.'

It is thus unsurprising that 'work first' strategies are viewed with suspicion by the poverty advocacy community. End Child Poverty (n.d.) emphasises that 'the majority (59 per cent) of poor children live in a household where at least one adult works'. Child Poverty Action Group (2009: 33) argues:

> precarious jobs that do not fit well with family life generate stress for parents and children. Simply seeking to move people into jobs is not an adequate response to child poverty ... relying on a 'work-first' approach undermines parents' rights to choose how to balance parenting and work.

The Institute for Public Policy Research (2009: 12) also cautions:

> There is much truth in the Government's claim that work is the best route out of poverty. However, the relationship between work and poverty is neither certain nor straightforward, and too many families in the UK are simply swapping one kind of poverty for another when they move into work.

The *Guardian* (2009) summarises such concerns, noting that 'the majority of children living in poverty now have at least one parent in work, but they are earning so little they are unable to drag their family above the poverty line', which 'runs counter to the government's message that work is the best route out of poverty'.

For the US context, Mead (2004: 51) noted that the adoption

of a 'work first' approach took a long time because 'most intellectuals ... view work as a threat to poor families'. This may not describe the position of the UK's poverty advocacy community, whose emphasis is on government policies to improve skill levels, 'create' better-paid jobs and provide more childcare services. But labour market incentives are clearly not part of their focus.

The government attempted to square this circle via the use of 'in-work benefits', especially the Child Tax Credit (CTC), a child-contingent means-tested benefit, and Working Tax Credit (WTC), a work-contingent means-tested benefit.[1] In adopting these instruments, it was recognised that traditional redistributive tools had weakened recipients' incentives to enter the labour market (HM Treasury, 2000). This was a sound premise because the traditional income replacement instruments such as Income Support, Jobseeker's Allowance and Incapacity Benefit had indeed a heavy anti-employment bias. If recipients had some earnings of their own, these were either fully counted against their benefits or they disqualified the recipient from entitlement to the benefit altogether. This practice was tantamount to a marginal income tax rate of 100 per cent or above. Thus, traditional redistributive elements could undermine future earning capacities and thereby perpetuate the problem they were intended to solve. Instead of addressing these problems within the existing income replacement schemes, i.e. reforming instruments such as Income Support, Jobseeker's Allowance and Incapacity Benefits, the government chose to add a second layer of benefits to correct

1   Child Tax Credit contains several layers. The 'Family Element' is a flat payment per family which is only withdrawn beyond a threshold of £50,000, so this element cannot reasonably be called 'means-tested'. It is a de facto universal benefit like Child Benefit. Both WTC and CTC contain top-ups for selected groups such as disabled workers or children.

the anti-work bias created by the first one. In-work benefits were different insofar as they could either be combined with work, as the Child Tax Credit is, or were even conditional on a minimum number of hours worked, as the Working Tax Credit is. They would top up small earnings and thereby restore work incentives (ibid.). Work-contingent benefits were seen as a form of government support which would not crowd out self-help, but rather 'crowd it in', because before it is paid out, some self-help effort is required from the recipient. The reimbursement of childcare costs was extended and the minimum wage introduced with the same motivation: these measures were expected to improve the living standards of low-paid workers in absolute terms, but also to make low-paid work more attractive relative to not working.

In-work benefits to top up wages had existed before, but they had played a minor role. In the mid-to-late 1990s, fewer than 5 per cent of all households headed by a working-age person received the indirect predecessor of Working Tax Credit and Child Tax Credit, the 'Family Credit'. Subsequently, coverage of tax credits was extended by loosening eligibility criteria, raising the initial rate, and lowering the rate at which they are withdrawn as earnings rise. Receipt of WTC and/or in-work CTC spread to 12 per cent of all working-age families by 2004 (New Policy Institute & Joseph Rowntree Foundation, n.d.). By 2010, 26.5 per cent of all children in the UK lived in working households receiving CTC and WTC; another 11.5 per cent lived in working households receiving CTC only, while a further 22 per cent lived in workless households receiving CTC or a close equivalent (based on data from Office for National Statistics & HM Revenue and Customs, 2010). Annual spending on WTC and CTC represents £20 billion, excluding WTC payments to households without children and excluding the near-universal component of CTC (based on data from Office for National Statistics & HM Revenue and Customs, 2009: 7). While CTC and WTC remain means-tested in a technical sense, it is debatable whether this term is still meaningfully applicable when the circle of recipients contains 60 per cent of a target population.[2]

The effects of these and other benefit reforms on labour market incentives have been analysed extensively by Adam et al. (2006), Blundell (2001), Brewer and Browne (2006), Brewer and Shephard (2004), Brewer et al. (2006b) and Brewer (2009). The extension of in-work benefits to top up low pay should lead to a fall in replacement ratios, the ratio of non-work income to in-work income with a low-paid job. The former consists of all benefit income which is not conditional on work; the latter of employment income minus taxes and National Insurance contributions (NIC) plus benefits that can be received while in work. For single parents, one of the key target groups of this reform, the introduction of WTC did indeed lower the replacement ratio.

But work-contingent benefits, by design, do not reach the very poorest, who usually do not work at all. If work-contingent benefits form part of a strategy to increase employment, this does not pose a problem. But it makes them an alien element in a strategy designed to meet income-based poverty targets. The Child Poverty Action Group (2009: 24) fully recognised this conflict:

> although we have a commitment to end child poverty, children who have parents who are not in work have family incomes well below the poverty line. Some children will always have parents who are unable to work. So if the 2020

2   This excludes the non-means-tested component of CTC, the Family Element. Including it would result in a coverage rate of 80 per cent of the child population.

> vision [of abolishing child poverty] is to be a reality, the
> value of out-of-work incomes must rise.

This incongruence of aims may explain why the government adopted policies that would appear contradictory to an outside observer. On the one hand, work-contingent benefits increased, lowering the replacement ratio and thus making employment relatively more attractive. On the other hand, benefits that could be claimed regardless of employment status, mostly child-contingent ones, were raised alongside these, raising the replacement ratio and thus making employment relatively less attractive again.[3]

The combined effect of all tax and benefit changes between 1997 and 2004, the period during which the important welfare reforms fell, was a fall in the replacement ratio for the 'median single parent' from 72 to 66 per cent. Half of all single parents fell into a band of replacement rates between 52 and 80 per cent, compared with 56 and 82 per cent at the beginning of the period (Brewer and Shephard, 2004: 26).

So, on balance, the opportunity cost of not working at all has gone up, but this effect could have been much more pronounced if the increase in work-contingent benefits had not been partially offset by increases in other benefits. Between the mid-1990s and the mid-2000s, the employment rate of single parents has risen

---

3   This point is denied by Child Poverty Action Group (2009: 25), which claims that '[t]he work disincentive argument is even weaker now than in the past. Child tax credit can be claimed in and out of employment, so increasing it does not act as a work disincentive.' But of course, if non-work income is 100 gold coins while in-work income is 200 gold coins, then introducing a universal lump sum of 50 gold coins will raise the replacement ratio from 100/200 = 50% to (100 + 50)/(200 + 50) = 60 per cent.

by ten percentage points, and structural labour market models suggests that work-contingent benefits have been a main contributor. But they also find that simultaneous changes in other parts of the tax and benefit system have partially undone the effect (Blundell, 2001; Brewer et al., 2006a). According to one model, the expansion of work-contingent benefits in isolation would have increased the employment rate of single mothers by 5.1 percentage points, but the simultaneous expansion of other benefits decreased it again by 1.5 percentage points. For other family types, outcomes have been less favourable. Looking at all working-age households with children, as many as three-quarters of the initial employment-boosting effects that would have arisen from work-contingent benefits in isolation have been offset by other changes in the benefit system. Promoting employment within an overall strategy aimed at a relative poverty target is like running up a 'down escalator'.

The sixteen-hours trap

The greatest problem with targeted benefits, work-contingent or not, is that they have to be withdrawn eventually as income rises. Withdrawing benefits effectively acts like a second income tax. For an individual deciding whether or not to work an additional hour, at a gross rate of £10 per hour, it makes no difference whether £2.50 is taken in tax, or whether entitlement to a benefit is reduced by £2.50 as a consequence. In both cases, the *effective* marginal tax rate (EMTR) is 25 per cent. EMTRs in Britain are, on average, not excessive by international standards. But the high rates which do arise are strongly concentrated, and often imposed on those who are least able to shoulder them.

The single most common EMTR, which most people working in the UK are confronted with, is 31 per cent: the basic rate of income tax plus employee contributions to National Insurance (NICs). There may be small additional deductions, but for three-quarters of the UK's working adults, the EMTR is below 40 per cent, with almost all of these falling into the 30–40 per cent range (Adam et al., 2006). About a tenth of working adults, however, are confronted with EMTRs above 60 per cent, many of them well above this level. Ironically, this tenth mainly consist of the weakest groups in the labour market. Excessive rates of this kind occur when people are liable to pay taxes and NICs, and benefits are withdrawn at the same time. Tax credits are withdrawn at a rate of 39 per cent for each additional gross £1 earned. Since the threshold beyond which tax credits are withdrawn is *below* the personal allowance, this results in an EMTR of 70 per cent, the sum of 31 per cent in explicit and 39 per cent in implicit taxes. Similarly, housing benefits are withdrawn at a rate of 65 per cent for each additional net £1 earned. This would result in an EMTR of 76 per cent, the sum of 31 per cent in explicit and 45 per cent in implicit taxes. But since Housing Benefit usually comes with Council Tax Benefit, which is itself withdrawn at a rate of 20 per cent for each additional £1 of net income earned, the typical EMTR for working recipients of Housing Benefit is closer to 90 per cent (see Table 20).

It is notable that for single parents, situations such as these are not the exception but the rule. Looking at the distribution of EMTRs among single parents, the median rate is about 70 per cent. Also, among working parents with a workless partner, the median EMTR is above 40 per cent, and thus somewhat above the rates that the vast majority of the working population deal with

(Brewer and Shephard, 2004: 33). It is also worth noting that the costs of working (travel-to-work costs and so on) tend to be fixed costs: they are therefore a bigger proportion of the net gain from working for those who face high EMTRs.

Table 20 **Increase in disposable income for an increase in gross earnings of £10 for various tax/benefit combinations**

Taxes/benefit withdrawal	Increase in disposable income	EMTR
Basic rate of income tax (IT) + National Insurance contributions (NIC)	£7.10	31%
IT + NIC + tapering of Council Tax Benefit (CTB)	£5.50	45%
IT + NIC + tapering of Working Tax Credit and/or Child Tax Credit (WTC/CTC)	£3.00	70%
IT + NIC + tapering of HB & CTB	£1.00	90%
IT + NIC + tapering of WTC/CTC, HB & CTB	£0.40	96%

If differential marginal tax rates were imposed upon two randomly selected groups, which do not differ systematically in variables such as education levels and work experience – say, 30 per cent on people whose surname begins with an 'M', and 70 per cent on people whose surname begins with an 'N' – then one would surely expect the economic outcomes of these groups to differ systematically after a number of years. In the M-group, a higher proportion of those who worked part-time at the beginning of the period would have moved on to full-time work. Members of the M-group would have switched to more demanding, better-paid positions more often, would have invested more in upgrading their skills, and there would be a greater prevalence of dual-earner households among them. Surely, any strategy that would leave the differential regime in place, but which would attempt to fight its consequences through granting selective subsidies or devising special work incentive schemes for the N-group, would be dismissed as a fight against a multi-headed hydra.

Yet there is no reason to expect otherwise if differential marginal tax rates are implicit rather than explicit. The above reasoning would apply a fortiori if the groups had not been chosen randomly, but if the high-EMTR group had been characterised by lower levels of education and work experience at the beginning of the period, and/or if people in that group were more responsive to adverse incentives.

As far as incentives at the margin are concerned, the welfare reforms enacted since the late 1990s, especially the expansion of in-work benefits, have replaced one undesirable state of affairs with another undesirable state of affairs. Broadly speaking, under the pre-1997 welfare system, means-tested benefits were generally withdrawn at steep rates. This kept the circle of benefit recipients smaller, but for a small group of working parents it made entry into or small advancements within the labour market virtu-ally irrational, at least in pecuniary terms. By making benefits 'portable' into working life, and by reducing the taper rates, the reforms of the last decade have reduced the number of people confronted with extremely high EMTRs. But by enlarging the circle of benefit recipients, there are now many more people who are on some kind of taper in the first place. In other words, the poverty trap has become less gluey for those entangled in it, but it has also grown in size and entangles greater numbers to begin with.

Previous recipients of Family Credit who are now recipients of WTC/CTC have seen their EMTRs fall because the taper rate of WTC/CTC is generally lower.[4] But while 4.8 per cent of all working-age households received Family Credit in 1999, 13.6 per cent received CTC or WTC/CTC in 2010. On the whole, there has been a decline in the number of working parents facing EMTRs above 80 per cent by about 5 per cent. But there has been an increase of more than 20 per cent in the number of working parents facing EMTRs between 50 and 80 per cent.

These policies have had their successes. A number of parents who were previously economically inactive are now in some form of employment. But few have moved beyond a small number of hours, so the increase in the number of parents who receive most of their income through wages and salaries has been modest. Notably, half of all single parents receiving WTC work at or just above the minimum threshold required to qualify for entitlement to WTC (Office for National Statistics & HM Revenue and Customs, 2010). The progress that has been achieved in raising the living standards of poor families with children has not developed a momentum. It remains dependent on continuous injections of large sums of government money. Supporters of redistributive policies saw this very clearly. Child Poverty Action Group (2009: 17) notes: 'Before 2005, the Government redistributed significantly towards lower income families with children via child tax credit … When, in 2005/06 and 2006/07, the Government did less, poorer families again fell behind and poverty rose.' Sefton et al. (2009: 33) add:

---

4   The two are not fully comparable because the Family Credit (FC) taper of 70 per cent was applied to net income while the WTC taper of 39 per cent is applied to gross income. For somebody paying 33 per cent in income tax and NIC, FC withdrawal would have meant an EMTR of 33 per cent + 70 per cent of 67 per cent = 80 per cent. The combination of income tax, NIC and WTC withdrawal usually leads to an EMTR of 70 per cent.

When the government has increased the child element of the CTC by more than earnings, as it did in April 2004 and 2008, this does have a noticeable impact on the net incomes of low earners. But, to maintain the early progress on child poverty, increases of this magnitude would have to be implemented every year.

The benefit maze

The benefit system's sheer complexity is itself part of the poverty trap. A high level of complexity was already present well before the adoption of the child poverty targets, so it is not the product of any particular social policy strategy. But the approach of adding an additional layer of benefits on top of the existing ones, instead of reforming the latter, has certainly not simplified matters. Martin (2009) documents that

> the DWP issues a total of 14 manuals, with a total of 8,690 pages, to its decision makers to help them to apply DWP benefits. A separate set of four volumes totalling over 1,200 pages covers Housing and Council Tax Benefits, which are primarily the responsibility of local authorities. The Tax Credits manual used by HM Revenue and Customs is a further 260 pages. (Ibid.)

Complexity, the author shows, arises in various ways:

- In the administration of the different types of benefits, there are differing definitions of key terms such as 'gainful employment' and 'income', and different accounting periods.
- Different benefits have different eligibility criteria, different maximum permissible thresholds for own income, savings and assets, and different withdrawal rates.

- There is a complex relationship between the various overlapping benefit types. Some benefits are mutually exclusive. Others can be combined, but may be partially counted against one another. Yet others are complementary, with the receipt of one being a precondition for the receipt of the other.
- A given condition which entitles somebody to support is often met with a mix of different transfer instruments. Condition 'X' does not simply entitle one to the receipt of 'X-benefit'. Rather, it will entitle a person to a package, consisting of an 'X-premium' added to the amount of another benefit, a higher threshold for the withdrawal of yet another benefit, and a lower withdrawal rate for yet another benefit. The condition 'disability', for example, is not simply met with a sufficiently large single transfer, but with differential treatment in the receipt of tax credits, Housing Benefit, Council Tax Benefit, Income Support and Jobseeker's Allowance. The condition 'parenthood' does not just entitle one to Child Tax Credit, Child Benefit and other child-contingent transfers, but also to premiums in the receipt of Housing Benefit and Council Tax Benefit.

This means that the gains from moving into employment, or from advancing farther once in minor employment, are not only small but also *uncertain*. For a recipient, complex interactions between different benefit elements make it hard to predict the exact pay-off from actions such as adding another day of work, or switching to a slightly better-paid position.

The precise impact of this uncertainty is unknown. But, at least in product markets, it has been shown empirically that uncertainty and high information costs foster inertia (e.g. Madrian and Shea, 2001). Potentially beneficial courses of actions are not undertaken. If this inertia effect is present in the benefit system as well, then disincentive effects do not just arise from a high average EMTR levied on benefit recipients, but also from a high standard deviation from this average. A benefit system with a single EMTR of x per cent would then, other things being equal, always be preferable to a multi-rate system with an average EMTR of x per cent.

It is also reasonable to assume that burdensome paperwork requirements create an 'endowment effect': benefit entitlement, once gained, is open-ended, which is unlikely to be the case for an initial job offer. This means that even if a recipient knows that taking up a job offer will result in an economic improvement, the improvement need not be long lived, and could well be followed by another lengthy benefit application procedure.

Encouragingly, the Department for Work and Pensions (2010) has recently released a paper which explicitly recognised the system's burdensome complexity and the work-discouraging effects arising from it. There is a good chance that the Conservative–Liberal coalition will address this issue at least partially.

Couple penalties

A straightforward way (at least in pecuniary terms) of exiting poverty is to form a common household with a partner. Larger households enjoy economies of scale in the use of housing space, domestic appliances and many other amenities. There is no need for the tax and benefit system to try to encourage joint household formation, but it should not be biased against this option, as the present system is. The bias arises from a split in the level of income assessment, with the tax liability being assessed at the individual level, and benefit eligibility being assessed at the household level. When, for example, a workless benefit recipient forms a joint household with a low-wage earner, the latter's income lowers the former's access to benefits, but the former's lack of income does not lower the latter's tax liability.

Again, this was already true before the adoption of the child poverty targets. But the more generous support of single parents has compounded the effect. Morgan (2007: 76–77) uses four representative case studies to show that the negative financial impact of declaring a relationship can be substantial. The author also provides an overview of the empirical literature on people's responsiveness to such (dis)incentives in terms of family structure and childbearing (ibid.: 96–121). While there is, unsurprisingly, disagreement on the magnitude of the responsiveness to pecuniary incentives in family formation, it is safe to say that the magnitude is not zero. Even in intimate decisions, economic incentives are not irrelevant.

15 TENETS OF AN ALTERNATIVE ANTI-POVERTY STRATEGY

The strategy adopted to meet the child poverty targets has achieved some useful outcomes. It has contributed to a higher employment rate among single parents and to a general reduction in the number of children living in workless households. But this modest success has come at a high fiscal cost. This chapter will sketch the outline of one possible anti-poverty strategy which is compatible with (though not dependent on) the understanding of poverty that underlies the Consensus Budget Standard Approach (CBSA) proposed earlier. This is not to say that a CBSA would be a one-way street towards the policies proposed here, or that these policy proposals are a novelty. It is merely an option that is very likely to be consistent, in emphasis and direction, with the CBSA. An underlying assumption is that the CBSA would have similar correlates with material deprivation measures.

Old-fashioned economic growth

In Rowntree's days, poverty meant hunger and cold. In 2008, in the midst of a severe economic downturn, people in the poorest decile (by gross equivalised income) were not only fed and clothed, but also managed to spare £700 for restaurants and hotels, £1,150 for recreation and culture, and £400 for communication services (based on data from Office for National Statistics, 2010a). This is the real fruit of long-term economic growth. Growth is good for the poor but modern poverty measurement has defined the fruit of economic progress away. A realistic poverty measure would not ignore the fact that growth raises the cost of social participation, but it would also not lose sight of the fact that the major force in favour of the poor is economic growth.

The poverty advocacy community usually ignores the benefits economic progress has achieved, and can still achieve, for the poor. This gives rise to regrettable misunderstandings. For example, the chief executive of CPAG, Kate Green, has recently embraced the views expressed by the authors of *The Spirit Level* (see Green, 2009). Yet contrary to what CPAG advocates, Wilkinson and Pickett (2009) explicitly reject the idea that improving the material comfort of the least well off could improve social problems in the developed world. Their central tenet is that absolute living standards in the developed world are fully sufficient, even at the lower end. This is surely a view which CPAG would vehemently oppose if it came from a different source. Wilkinson and Pickett illustrate their position by pointing to the high ownership rates of goods such as air conditioning, DVD players, cars or dishwashers among Americans below the domestic poverty line (Wilkinson and Pickett, 2010: 60). This is precisely the type of reasoning which poverty advocacy groups usually criticise as an attempt to 'define poverty away'.

The 'satiation point' beyond which growth becomes useless is myth. To future generations, our present standards of living will appear just as hopelessly inadequate as the living standards of Rowntree's days appear to us. The conventional growth-enabling strategy of low and simple taxes, open markets (domestically and internationally), light and limited statutory regulation, the rule of law and sound legal institutions, free labour markets and monetary stability is still a strategy with a heavy pro-poor bias.

Competition, entrepreneurship, open markets

Within the present, largely income-based framework of poverty measurement, the policy focus on income supplementation seems natural. Arguably, supply-side reforms aimed at unleashing competition in the sectors that poor households most rely upon could have been more cost effective. Estimates by the Institute for Fiscal Studies (2008, 2009) decompose the UK's inflation rate of recent years into differential inflation rates, as faced by different population subgroups. They show that changes in the structure of relative prices can affect the level and distribution of purchasing power substantially. The poverty measures underlying the targets are generally blind to such changes. Indeed, the emergence of ersatz indicators dealing with specific deprivations, such as 'Poverty After Housing Costs' and 'Fuel Poverty', can be interpreted as an attempt to compensate for these blind spots. A more consistent approach, of course, would be to find a primary measure of poverty which is able to detect these developments to begin with.

There is certainly scope for enhanced price competition and entrepreneurship in a number of sectors. Estimates by Oxford Economic Forecasting (2005) show that a liberalisation of agricultural and textile markets, especially with regard to foreign trade, would lead to falling prices in these markets even in the short term. They also show that poor households would benefit more than proportionately.

Proposals for more market-based solutions in the provision of utilities have been around for a long time (e.g. Robinson, 2001; Hunt, 2003). They have seldom been specifically presented as a tool for poverty reduction, but rather as a strategy for using the 'discovery process' function of markets. As a desirable side effect, however, price falls in these markets would have a strong pro-poor bias, and a CBSA poverty measure would identify it. On average, households in the poorest decile spend 30 per cent of their budget on food and non-alcoholic drinks, electricity, gas, fuel and water charges. People in the fifth decile spend about 20 per cent on these items, and people in the upper decile 10 per cent (based on data from the Office for National Statistics, 2010a).

The good to which these considerations apply most is housing. An across-the-board fall (rise) in the cost of housing would have a much stronger pro-poor (anti-poor) bias than a change in the cost of any other good. High housing costs affect the poor in many ways, as they have knock-on effects in the form of high commercial rents feeding through into higher retail prices. If the poor lack a car, they may not be able to shop in cheaper, out-of-town areas. So arguably, the single most effective anti-poverty measure would be one that enables a drastic fall in the cost of housing.

The exceptionally high housing costs in the UK are often blamed on a high population density. Yet with 250 inhabitants per km2, population density in the UK is lower than in West Germany,[1] Belgium (350/km2) and the Netherlands (485/km2) (Eurostat, online database). Nevertheless, between the 1970s and the early 2000s, residential property prices in the UK increased 3.5-fold in real terms, compared with a 2.5-fold increase in the Netherlands, a doubling in Belgium, and no increase in Germany

---

1   German population density is 230/km2, heavily skewed towards the west.

Figure 12 **Housing costs in the UK as a percentage of equivalised disposable incomes, selected income percentiles**

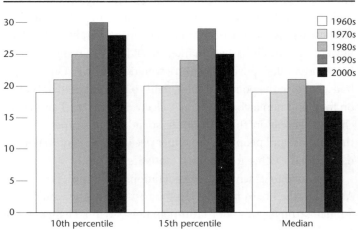

Source: Based on data from Institute for Fiscal Studies (2010)

(Evans and Hartwich, 2005: 23). The excessive cost of living space and commercial space in the UK is caused by a highly restrictive land-use planning system, effectively a quantity control that holds housing supply artificially scarce while demand for it is burgeoning (ibid.). Housing is a basic requirement; one should expect its share in households' budgets to fall over time. In the UK, the opposite has happened for those farther down the income distribution.

It could be argued that Figure 12 overstates the problem because most low-income households do not actually pay the cost of housing out of their net income – 18 per cent of households are in receipt of Housing Benefit (Office for National Statistics &

Department for Work and Pensions, 2009b). But this aggravates the problem rather than diminishes it. Housing Benefit provides a very strong anti-work disincentive, since it is withdrawn at a rate of 65 per cent as recipients' net earnings rise. Especially in high-rent areas, it is notoriously difficult for low-skilled workers to fully compensate for housing benefits through their own earnings. In Inner London, as many as 30 per cent of households receive Housing Benefit (ibid.).

In short, one could hardly think of a more effective anti-poverty policy than a thorough liberalisation of the planning system, with the aim of substantially reducing the cost of housing through supply-side adjustment. The effect cannot be quantified since no counterfactual to the present planning regime, other things being equal, is available. But in reviewing the empirical literature on the relationship between house prices and local variations in the planning system, Corkindale (2004: 83–5) finds that even within the UK, housing is noticeably cheaper where planning restrictions are less excessive. Proposals for a denationalisation of the planning system have been put forward by Pennington (2002).

As a second-best solution,[2] the granting of development permits could be entirely placed within the hands of municipalities, accompanied by fiscal decentralisation. This would change the incentive structure facing local electorates: releasing land for residential or commercial development would increase local tax revenue, enabling better local public services and/or lower local tax rates. At present, local residents receive no tangible benefit from building activities in their area. This means that a pressure

2   Pennington's first-best solution consists of transferring the right to grant development permits to private companies, which could be owned by local residents.

group of local residents which manages to prevent a building project receives the full benefit (a lower population density), but does not bear the cost of their action (the forgone tax revenue). All the political incentives are biased against building. Unfortunately, the planning policy of the Conservative–Liberal coalition thus far would strengthen this asymmetry. It strengthens local authorities' powers to block the release of land for building, while leaving the anti-building bias in the fiscal structure intact. It has been labelled a 'recipe for nimbyism' (Economist, 2010a).

It is notable that poverty advocacy groups hardly, if ever, cover these aspects of poverty. They do refer to overcrowding and poor housing conditions. But they either present them as just another consequence of poverty or they take present conditions as given and call upon the government to provide extra-market solutions such as social housing. Their primary focus is on income and its distribution. This leads to the strange situation that poverty advocacy groups ignore tangible obstacles which the poor face, such as the anti-poor bias in the planning system, while at the same time venturing into areas which are at best remotely poverty related, such as executive pay, top marginal tax rates and inheritance taxes (e.g. Child Poverty Action Group, 2009; Toynbee, 2008). Furthermore, simply providing housing subsidies – while fixing supply – puts further upward pressure on house prices at the expense of those who may be in the lower deciles but not in receipt of housing benefit.

Removing poverty traps

Weak labour market attachment, unsurprisingly, is identified as a poverty risk by any poverty measure. But the magnitude of this risk factor is higher when poverty is measured by the material deprivation measure, especially for lone parents. Looking at an econometric model decomposing relative poverty and material deprivation rates into their explanatory factors, it shows that 'living in a workless lone-parent family increases the likelihood of being in poverty on both measures, but the impact is much larger for material deprivation than it is for income (37.6% against 21.7%)' (Brewer et al., 2008a: 76).

Since the Consensual Budget Standard Approach is a measure of material deprivation, it would most likely provide a case for 'work-first' policies as well. The often heard claim that most poor children live in working households is a half-truth. It reflects the fact that government policies of the last decade have provided parents, particularly single parents, with stronger incentives to take up sixteen hours of work per week to qualify for Working Tax Credit. But extending working hours from this level is usually not lucrative in pecuniary terms. These households are not, strictly speaking, unemployed, but they are not economically self-supporting either. Looking at children living with couples, about 2.2 million belong to a household that falls in the bottom income quintile after housing costs; 1.6 million of them live in a household in which at least one member is in some form of employment. This includes 0.4 million children belonging to a self-employed household, however, and the inappropriateness of using income data for groups with volatile incomes has already been discussed. Another 0.3 million children live in lower-income-couple households where nobody works full-time. Children in households where both adults work, and at least one of them works full-time, account for just 0.2 million of this quintile.

Of the 3.1 million children living with single parents, 1.4 million belong to a household that falls in the bottom income quintile after housing costs, but only about 0.1 million out of these live in a household headed by a full-time worker (based on data from Office for National Statistics & Department for Work and Pensions, 2009a: 61).

When looking at the dynamics instead of the snapshot, even the relative standard, which poverty activists usually prefer, provides no strong case against a work-first approach (ibid.: 66). The share of children living in households experiencing persistent low income after housing costs stood at 15 per cent in 2004–07. The rate for households where all adults work was 6 per cent, compared with 12 per cent in households where one adult works and one does not and 49 per cent in households where no adult works. Looking at those below the relative poverty line in any given year, the share of those who will cross the poverty line within the next year is eleven to thirteen percentage points higher among the 'working poor' than among the non-working poor (ibid.: 55–6). This is consistent with the long-established finding that labour market detachment perpetuates itself, and leads to a vicious circle of skills depreciation and decreased employment prospects (e.g. Pissarides, 1992).

As mentioned, the case for putting work first is strongest when measuring poverty by material deprivation, which decreases as the household's degree of labour market attachment increases.

It can be inferred from this that a CBSA approach would also lend support to work-first policies. In addition, long-term detachment from the labour market has been found to be related to a variety of mental health problems, contributing to a multitude of social ills (Kay, 2010: 21–4). As such, a strategy for a profound reform of welfare could be based on the principles expounded below.

Table 21 **Material deprivation rates for children by employment status of their parents**

Economic (and family) status of household	Material deprivation poverty rate
Couple – both work full-time	1%
Couple – one works full-time, one part-time	2%
Lone parent in full-time work	7%
Couple – single full-time breadwinner	13%
All children (average)	17%
Lone parent in part-time work	21%
Couple, no full-time worker, one (or more) part-time worker	34%
Workless couple	51%
Workless lone parent	58%

Source: Statistics from Office for National Statistics & Department for Work and Pensions (2009a)

Lower effective marginal tax rates

Labour market models show that labour supply elasticities are highest among the low-skilled and, in particular, among single mothers (Blundell et al., 1998; Meghir and Phillips, 2008). So if a case for differential effective marginal tax rates were to be made at all, then it would be a case for *lower* effective marginal tax rates on the most vulnerable groups. The present system does the precise opposite. It levies the highest effective marginal tax rates on those groups that are most likely to be held back by them. Therefore, the present system does not unlock poor people's own capacities for self-improvement.

Benefit simplification

The Department for Work and Pensions (2010: 19–24) has presented a far-reaching proposal to merge Income Support, Jobseeker's Allowance, Employment and Support Allowance, Housing Benefit, Council Tax Benefit, Working Tax Credit and Child Tax Credit into a 'Universal Credit' with a single taper rate. This would go a long way in the right direction. In the current system, however, complexity arises not just because there are different types of benefits, but also because each of these benefits has numerous special provisions of its own. The DWP paper does not explain whether these, too, will be standardised, or whether they will be maintained and merely united under a common roof. In the latter case, the Universal Credit could itself become a hugely complex instrument, albeit, of course, somewhat better than the present system.

Martin (2009) proposes a multi-stage plan for benefit simplification which goes farther. It would begin with a standardisation of variables such as the assessment base. Overlaps would then be eliminated, unwinding and rearranging the different components of existing benefits, so that one instrument is assigned to one condition. Benefits that serve similar purposes would be merged, and so would income tax and National Insurance contributions. Since National Insurance benefits do not follow genuine insurance principles, National Insurance is de facto nothing but a second income tax combined with an employer's payroll tax anyway. A comparable proposal for benefit simplification has been brought forward by the Institute for Fiscal Studies under the header of 'Integrated Family Support' (Brewer et al., 2008b: 54–60).

While going a long way towards deactivating the poverty trap, even these proposals would not eliminate the complexity and adverse incentive effects that arise from the interaction of the benefit system with the tax system. So a possible extension of the above proposals would be a complete separation of tax liability and benefit entitlement, through converting benefits into a Friedmanite Negative Income Tax. Every household would either pay income tax or receive income-related benefits, but never both at the same time. Moving towards a negative income tax would require additional tax-free allowances for children, which can be financed through lowering child-contingent benefits. A negative income tax that replaces all benefits would bring down the highest effective marginal tax rates, substantially reduce complexity and eliminate anti-work distortions. It would also eliminate a major proportion of 'welfare churning', the practice of redistributing from people's right-hand pocket to their left-hand pocket.

Removing couple penalties

Since the formation of a joint household with a partner can be a comparatively easy way out of poverty, removing disincentives against doing so is low-hanging fruit. A way of achieving this is to make the tax-free personal allowance transferable between two partners and to introduce an additional tax-free allowance for each child in a household – this can all be done within a negative income tax system.

The policy aim should not be to consciously 'promote' family formation, which cannot be the role of the state in a free society. But tax liability and benefit entitlement have to be assessed at *some* level, either the individual or the household, and none of these options will be entirely 'neutral' as far as its behavioural incentives are concerned. The present splitting, with tax liability and benefit entitlement being assessed at different levels, has turned out to be highly intrusive in interfering with personal choices. So, arguably, choosing one level of assessment, either the individual or the household, and maintaining it both for tax and benefit purposes, would be the less intrusive approach. Since it is hardly sensible to extend benefit eligibility to non-working spouses of wealthy individuals, assigning tax-free allowances to households instead of to individuals is a moderate proposal. This issue may be addressed by the present coalition government, though the two parties have differing views on this matter.

School choice

It does not need to be pointed out that low educational attainment constitutes a poverty risk. But again, the magnitude of this risk factor relative to others tends to be greater when looking at hardship/deprivation measures than when looking at income poverty measures (Brewer et al., 2009a: 173). The UK's education system fails students from poor backgrounds and it leaves large numbers of people without the skills required in the modern labour market. Parental and school background exert a higher influence on individual educational attainment than in many other developed countries, leading to an unusually high educational polarisation (see Table 22). This perpetuates aspects of inequality which do not arise from differences in personal preferences, inherent talents and voluntary decisions.

A school choice model under which funding would follow the pupil, even to a non-state school, is presently being discussed and partially implemented in the UK. The impact of such a quasi-voucher scheme on poor pupils in particular can go either way.

Table 22 **Educational outcomes**

	Index of the influence of parental background on student achievement (0–100)	School environment effect index (0–100)	Functional illiteracy, % of the population aged 16–65	% of the population aged 25–64 with below upper secondary educational attainment
Denmark	39	16	9.6	25
Austria	43	30	n. a.	20
Canada	33	21	14.6	13
Sweden	38	15	7.5	15
Germany	47	77	14.4	16
Spain	31	16	n. a.	49
USA	49	31	20.0	12
Britain	48	34	21.8	32

Source: Statistics from OECD (2010, 2009), United Nations Development Programme (2009)

It has the potential of raising educational standards through the injection of competition into the school system. This should benefit students from low-education backgrounds most, because they are less able to access substitutes to compensate for the education system's deficiencies. Critics, on the other hand, fear that only the most ambitious parents would take up the opportunity to set up schools of their own. Pupils from privileged backgrounds would be pulled out of the state schools, leaving others behind with a weaker peer group (Campaign for State Education, n.d.; Anti Academies Alliance, n.d.). The relative impact on students from different backgrounds would depend on the extent to which the newly emerging non-state-school sector would rely on parents' idealism alone. Forster (2008) examines the evidence

from regional voucher pilot projects in the USA, which constitute (unintentional) natural experiments since the programmes
are usually oversubscribed and vouchers are allocated by lottery.
Applicants who did not receive a voucher thus represent a control
group; distorting factors such as the parents' educational background, parental ambition and access to private supplementary
tuition ought to hold constant. It shows that students from disadvantaged backgrounds gain more, not less, than their privileged
peers. The reason for this may well be that the better off already
have pretty effective mobility between schools of different quality
because of the ability to move house or (in some cases) purchase
private education.

Work requirements

The anti-poverty package outlined here contains an element which
involves an unpleasant trade-off. High elasticity of labour supply
at the lower end of the income distribution provides a strong
case for cutting EMTRs drastically in this range. Lowering withdrawal rates of benefits, however, would also extend eligibility for
benefits to ranges farther up the income distribution. The benefit
system would become less targeted, putting large numbers of non-
needy recipients on benefit rolls. A poorly targeted benefit system
is incompatible with the aim of low taxation. It would also crowd
out private insurance of savings-based provision for those who are
perfectly able to provide for themselves.

The nature of this trade-off can be illustrated by imagining a
simplified negative income tax system, where an initial amount
for zero earners is withdrawn, as the recipient's earnings grow,
at a constant rate. The basic income is assumed to be £700 per

month, which is roughly the sum of the standard rate of Income Support plus a rather low level of Housing Benefit, ignoring Council Tax Benefit and any other possible payments. When there is no income disregard and no other factor to observe then, at a withdrawal rate of 60 per cent, a household would need equivalised earnings[3] above the median income to come fully off benefits. So, at a 60 per cent rate, the system would not be highly targeted, and the EMTR would still be higher than top marginal tax rates in Denmark and Sweden. If withdrawal rates were set as low as 31 per cent, as would be required if they are not to exceed EMTRs on median incomes, then even people in the highest income brackets would qualify for benefits – see Table 23.

Table 23 **Break-even points for various benefit withdrawal rates**

Monthly benefit payout	Withdrawal rate	'Break-even point' (= monthly income at which benefit is fully tapered away)	Percentile range of the equivalised income distribution containing break-even point
£700	100%	£700	15th–25th
£700	80%	£875	35th–40th
£700	60%	£1,167	55th–65th
£700	50%	£1,400	65th–70th
£700	40%	£1,750	75th–85th
£700	31%	£2,258	90th–95th

The Liberal–Conservative coalition has thus far ignored this basic trade-off. It simultaneously declared its intentions to improve work incentives at the margin *and* to make the transfer

---

3   Using the McClements equivalence scale, which attaches a weight of 0.61 to a household's first adult, this household's equivalised income would be £1,167/0.61 = £1,913. The equivalised median income is £1,765.

system more targeted, without addressing the conflict between these two aims. The Department for Work and Pensions (2010) outlines its welfare reform strategy:

Reforms could:

- improve work incentives by reforming the way in which benefits are tapered as incomes rise and allow people to keep more of their earnings;
- be fair and targeted to those most in need through tapers which focus payments on those on the lowest incomes, while maintaining levels of support for those out of work. (Ibid.: 38)

So how can a benefit system target its payments towards those most in need, provide reasonably high benefit levels and still withdraw them at low rates? A way to square this circle would be to condition the receipt of in-work benefits on full-time work, and to attach work requirements to payments made to recipients outside the formal labour market.

Work requirements have been operative in the US state of Wisconsin since the mid-1980s. Following the 1996 'Personal Responsibility and Work Act', they have been expanded US-wide, but generally in a much less consistent way. Although sometimes taken to be the same thing (e.g. Guardian, 2010), Wisconsin-style workfare goes far beyond the 'conditionality' the Department for Work and Pensions (2010: 28–30) plans to expand. 'Workfare' essentially means that healthy recipients are expected to undergo work tests and engage in work for the local council or guided job search as a precondition for receiving benefits. Job offers have to be accepted. Payments are contingent on compliance, which is monitored by case managers. Ideally, a workfare regime is one in which the daily life of a benefit recipient is not very different from the daily life of their working peers. Like their employed neighbours, benefit recipients would get up in the morning and go about a structured occupation during the day.

In this chapter, workfare is not proposed as a stand-alone strategy, but as an ingredient of a work-focused anti-poverty strategy. It should form part of a completely new welfare system, in which there would be only two types of benefits for healthy people of working age: 'workfare' for people outside of formal employment, and a negative income tax (NIT) for people in low-paid full-time employment.

Part-time employees would no longer be in receipt of income top-ups from the taxpayer – at least not on an open-ended basis.[4] Single parents would receive help with childcare, but a workload approaching full-time employment would be expected of them as well.

As far as workfare is concerned, receiving the full benefit payment would be conditional on a workload not very different from that of a full-time job, with deductions being made for non-compliance. Therefore, there would be no reason not to look for a full-time job in the regular labour market straight away.

Workfare payments and the negative income tax could not be received at the same time. As such, once entering a regular full-time job, entitlement to workfare would be lost entirely. But low earnings from full-time work would be topped up because the difference between the market income and the tax-free threshold would be 'negatively taxed'.

---

4   Alternatively, part-time workers could qualify for NIT, but on the basis of the full-time equivalent earnings, so that shortening a five-day workweek to, say, two days would not increase the NIT payment. By the same token, this would mean that the withdrawal rate for extending a two-day to a five-day workweek is zero.

Debates about a workfare reform of some sort have been around in many places, including in the UK. They have thus far been led in unnecessarily emotional terms. Critics have interpreted the proposal as an implicit accusation that economic inactivity was a deliberately adopted lifestyle choice. In fact, the case for workfare requires no such assumption, and is even compatible with the opposite view. In this chapter, the case for workfare has been derived 'by default'. Access to benefits always has to be restricted in some way; there is no welfare system that grants unlimited access to benefit payments. For in-work benefits, this gatekeeper function can be performed either by taper rates or by minimum hour requirements. The present tax credit system uses a combination of both, but the emphasis is clearly on the former. If the first hurdle (taper rate) is to be lowered, and total welfare spending is not to increase, then the second hurdle (minimum hour requirements) has to go up. If Working Tax Credit and Child Tax Credit were merely replaced by a more coherent version of the former Family Credit, however, then many part-time working recipients would simply be pushed back into worklessness. This leaves workfare as an option.

There are sound, reasonable objections to workfare from several political camps. Yet the emphasis of this section is not on workfare per se, but on lowering effective marginal tax rates and thus reducing the poverty trap. There might be better ways of slashing these rates without increasing spending, but the burden of proof for this should be on the workfare critics.

Critics should also bear in mind that, as a desirable side effect, a workfare regime is also likely to improve the social standing of benefit recipients. This is relevant for the UK context because international surveys show that welfare recipients are held in significantly lower esteem here than in the rest of Europe. In the years preceding the financial crisis, just over half of the British population agreed with the statement that 'benefits for the unemployed are too high and discourage work', while two-thirds thought that 'most unemployed people could find a job if they really wanted one'. About a quarter of respondents blamed poverty on 'laziness and a lack of willpower', a view that is almost non-existent in places such as Sweden and East Germany (Sefton, 2009: 237–42). These attitudes would certainly be different with a properly implemented workfare system, in which a life 'on the dole' is not that different from a life off the dole. Tabloid sound bites of 'welfare scroungers' would become obsolete. The key beneficiaries would be those who are genuinely looking for regular employment, but cannot find it for whatever reason. They would also benefit from maintaining work-related habits, which would make the transition from formal employment into welfare and vice versa much smoother.

The success of workfare is not trivial. Over the latter half of the 1990s, the number of benefit claimants in Wisconsin dropped by more than 80 per cent. Economic conditions were favourable, but Mead demonstrates, by the use of both quantitative and qualitative evidence, that work requirements had a large impact of their own. An empirical labour market model (Mead, 1999) and a survey among key welfare administrators (Mead, 2004: 197–202) both point in this direction.

Mead also emphasises that a workfare regime places challenging demands on the welfare bureaucracy, and that correct implementation is crucial. The author documents the significant cross-county policy variations within Wisconsin, for example in the severity with which sanctions were applied, or in the trade-off between immediate work and training. These variations resulted from a high degree of local autonomy (ibid.: 79–106). This is probably where the difference between Wisconsin and the UK, with its tradition of centralised social policymaking, is greatest. A workfare policy centrally imposed from Whitehall would almost certainly be a failure. Tax credits, too, worked out differently 'on the ground' than they were supposed to in theory, and a reform of the system of incapacity benefits has been on the political agenda for a long time to no avail. Local autonomy has to be the key feature – but local autonomy is pointless without a significant degree of local cost-sharing, paid out of local taxation. Only 'Swiss-style' localism, where decision-making and fiscal responsibilities are allocated to the same level, provides proper accountability.

Reform interactions

Some of the above-mentioned reforms would best unfold their beneficial effects when implemented together. Apart from their direct effects on the wallets of the poor, lower costs of goods would also increase the effectiveness of welfare reform. In particular, a lower cost of housing would enable a reduction in housing benefit (or the housing cost component of a new benefit system) such that the non-employed are no worse off, and the low paid are better off. This would reduce the replacement ratio of benefit income to income from low-skilled employment, further improving incentives to enter the labour market. As a knock-on effect, effective marginal tax rates could also be cut further. The lower the initial sum paid out, the lower the taper rate can be. This would improve incentives to progress in the labour market. At present, the differential in the cost of housing also acts as a deterrent for people in economically weak areas to move to areas with better employment prospects. Nominal wages in London and other cities in the South-East may be high compared with, say, the North of England. But if the difference in housing costs eats up all the gain relocation ceases to be lucrative. Housing demand is most pressing in the areas where job market prospects are best. Enabling an increase in residential construction would cut the cost of housing most in these areas, leading to an improvement in living standards there, not just in absolute terms, but also relative to areas with fewer employment opportunities. The magnitude of this cannot be known, but labour market mobility within the country could only increase. A work-focused welfare reform would be most effective, of course, when moving into areas with high labour demand is a realistic option for many people.

Needless to say, increasing the supply of labour through welfare reform should ideally be matched with an increased demand for labour. A growing economy with a buoyant labour market does not, on its own, decrease measured poverty, as the decade from the late 1990s to the onset of the financial crisis has shown. But it provides the ideal framework for a work-focused welfare reform, as the Wisconsin experience has demonstrated.

Some would also argue that a significant improvement in the quality of schooling for the very poor would lead to better job prospects and a decreased likelihood that childbearing would take place at very young ages when the need for external financial support was at its greatest. This too then reduces the demand for certain types of welfare benefits.

16 CONCLUSION

We have travelled a long way from Seebohm Rowntree's days, when the lot of the poorest meant hunger, cold, illness and premature death. Today, amid a sharp economic downturn, the least well-off people in Britain can still afford a vast array of goods and services which, if they existed at all, represented luxuries to the better off a few generations ago. Washing machines and tumble dryers, refrigerators and freezers, microwaves, TVs and DVD players, computers and cameras, membership of sports and health clubs, attendance at concerts and sports events, foreign holidays including air travel and hotel stays, eating out, tropical fruits and wine, bank accounts and insurance products – consumption of these goods and services can nowadays be found even among the poorer members of society. This is the fruit of economic progress and there is no reason why this process should come to an end. The prevalence rates of these items among the poor can rise a lot higher still, and many additional goods and services can enter the list.

Nevertheless, poverty continues to concern us, as it should. At the same time, it would be absurd to claim that the improvements in the living conditions of the least well off have achieved nothing only because other people have enjoyed improvements to their living standards. But it is undeniable that Britain today is a very different society from the 1950s, let alone the 1890s. Poverty is still real today, even if it is understood differently. Poverty is context specific, at least to some extent, because the definition of necessities is context specific. There is nothing inherent in a telephone or a fridge which would make these goods 'necessities' or 'luxuries'. They are necessities in some places but not in others, depending on whether owners are required to participate in the social life and comply with the social conventions prevailing in a particular time and place. These goods were not necessities in the 1920s, but they are today. As societies grow wealthier, social norms and expectations become more demanding and social participation becomes more costly.

Earlier approaches to poverty measurement, in particular the 'Budget Standard Approach' which dominated poverty research in the first half of the twentieth century, have struggled to incorporate this dynamic, context-specific nature of poverty. This is because the approach originated as a measure of impeded physical functioning. When the developed world finally overcame this most basic form of deprivation, it looked as if the Budget Standard Approach had fulfilled its mission and become obsolete. Poverty then came to be seen as impeded social participation, a concept which the Budget Standard Approach seemed ill equipped to grasp. Relative measures emerged as an alternative that appeared to overcome this deficiency. The simplistic logic behind relative measures was that since they tagged the poverty line to median incomes, they must be 'rooted in their social context'. Researchers and the policy community began to read much more into the relative measure than it actually expressed. The relative poverty line came to be seen as an approximation of the cost of social participation, a yardstick for inclusion in or exclusion from a particular society. There was never any evidence that this was the case; one might as well have tagged the poverty line to an index of industrial production, or to a stock market index, and claim that this anchored it in a social context.

But relative measures go beyond merely producing random figures with little social relevance. Being a measure of inequality in the bottom half of the distribution, they divert all policy attention to the distribution of nominal incomes. They respond strongly to income transfers, but they cannot detect any side effects arising from them. Nor can they detect any changes in command over resources, as long as these arise outside the distribution of nominal incomes. They are completely detached from poor people's actual consumption patterns and the cost of the goods that poor people buy.

Relative measures now inform public opinion much more than any measures of specific deprivations, because the rates they produce are simply being reported as 'the number of people living in poverty'. This has given rise to a highly politicised landscape of anti-poverty campaign groups and NGOs. 'Poverty' measured in these terms ceases to be a problem confined to specific, identifiable groups, which would be addressable with a narrow set of targeted measures. Instead, it becomes a feature of the economic system as a whole. Any policy that might affect the income distribution now draws the attention of the advocacy community. Anti-poverty initiatives are no longer about 'narrow' issues such as overcrowded housing or poor learning conditions for pupils from disadvantaged backgrounds. Instead, 'systemic' issues come to the fore. Bankers' bonuses, executive pay, top income tax rates and inheritance tax, even globalisation and climate change come on the radar. The height of confusion is reached when poverty campaigners team up with 'spirit level egalitarians'. The latter advocate a forcible restriction of economic growth, and explicitly oppose further increases in the material comfort of the least well off.

Income-based relative poverty measures are also a poor guide to actual policies. Strategies to address child poverty targets in the UK are a case in point. Costly programmes of income redistribution have been adopted, while potentially more cost-effective, but politically more challenging, measures have been neglected. A wholesale liberalisation of the land-use planning system would hugely benefit the poor through various channels, in both relative and absolute terms. But unlike the income transfer strategy pursued over the last decade, it would cost the general taxpayer nothing. It would provide no adverse work incentives either, since the benefits of low-cost housing are not 'tapered away'. A similar logic applies to many other service and product markets, housing being merely the one in which the potential for 'pro-poor' supply-side policies is the largest – though the gains may be scarcely less from education reform.

Even when ignoring product and service markets altogether, income-based relative poverty targets can provide counterproductive policy signals. The precise design of tools such as tax credits is shaped by their purpose. If they are meant to provide stronger work incentives, it would be sensible to condition them strictly on work, or even full-time work. But this makes them unsuitable to meet a relative poverty target, because it would mean setting the bar rather high. But if the aim is to maximise take-up, then the bar would have to be set as low as possible, which means requiring no work effort from the recipient. The tax credit system introduced in the UK has been a confusing mix of both approaches.

The work-contingent component, Working Tax Credit, did

raise the employment rate of single parents, which was the lowest anywhere in Europe by a wide margin. But it did so at much greater fiscal cost than necessary, owing to offsetting effects created by other changes in the benefit system. Having tripled spending on in-work benefits in real terms, the UK still has the lowest employment rate of single parents in Europe, albeit now with a narrower distance to the second-lowest. Also, few of the new labour market entrants have become economically self-supporting. While incentives to enter the labour market in the first place have improved for some groups, incentives to work more or improve skills once in minor employment have not.

The shortcomings of relative indicators are not overcome by replacing them with 'absolute' measures, i.e. by unlinking the poverty line from median income and linking it to the Consumer Price Index instead. Such quasi-absolute measures would still be blind to changes in the product market, and they would still be heavily biased towards encouraging income transfers. This is because income can be directly and immediately affected by changes in the tax and benefit system whereas expenditure is much more inert. Reflecting not only momentary income, but also future expectations, expenditure is stubbornly unimpressed by policy changes in the short term. By the same token, this means that replacing an income-based measure with an expenditure-based measure would, to some extent, depoliticise poverty measurement. It would also avoid the bias against self-employment, and income volatility in general, that is inherent in income-based poverty measures.

So, if relative measures of poverty are unable to sensibly inform public opinion and policymaking, and absolute measures are not an alternative, then what is the best approach? In fact, a plausible alternative does exist. Poverty, albeit a highly abstract and vague concept, is not merely in the eye of the beholder. Measures of 'Consensual Material Deprivation', such as the Poverty and Social Exclusion Survey, reveal a surprising fact: people may fiercely disagree on what constitutes poverty when debating the topic in abstract terms. But when asked to identify tangible necessities, and demarcating them from items that are merely desirable, there is a surprisingly robust consensus. Of course there are controversial items and borderline cases. But, by and large, such deviations are random ones, instead of systematically differing across population subgroups. It is this consensus which should form the basis of a sensible poverty measure – one that approximates the true 'cost of social participation'.

Combining 'Consensual Material Deprivation' and the 'Budget Standard Approach' into an integrated poverty measure could well fulfil the promise that accompanied the ascent of relative measures – namely that they could produce a measure that is rooted in its social context. Like relative poverty indicators, this poverty line would rise over time. But it would not mechanically follow changes in median incomes.

Such a poverty measure would be a 'relative' of material deprivation measures. So from looking at the risk factors of material deprivation, as well as at the risk factors of expenditure poverty, it is already possible to draw up an alternative anti-poverty strategy, at least in outline. First of all, we would not deny the value of economic growth. If all incomes grow fast and social norms adjust only with a substantial time lag, then poverty could fall even if the income distribution widens. Increased inequality would not have an impact on the poverty measure per se. Similarly, in times of recession and higher unemployment we would not get the bizarre result that poverty was falling (because the incomes of the rich were falling more). If, in times of growth, the additional income growth enjoyed by median income earners vis-à-vis low income earners is channelled into the consumption of goods that have little impact on social norms, then poverty would not rise.

Structural changes in product markets could be reflected through the Budget Standard Approach element of the indicator. Items would regularly be replaced with suitable substitutes, and market prices frequently updated.

The measure we propose would also focus attention on the areas where tangible improvements for the least well off can be made in the most cost-effective way. Instead of being diverted by abstract aggregates, it would reveal which goods and services the poor find most difficult to access. The proportion of poor people's budgets spent on housing is still substantially higher than in the 1960s, a completely counter-intuitive development for a basic good. The excessive cost of housing is the result of a restrictive land use planning system driven by political rent-seeking behaviour.

Recent changes to the planning system may well increase the cost of housing further. While this negatively affects the poor in a very tangible way, no statement on this issue was released by the poverty advocacy community. Some of them preferred to continue writing about bankers' bonuses. Nor have issues such as agricultural protectionism in the EU, which also harms the poor in tangible ways through higher food prices, ever been on their agenda.

The largest risk for material hardship, as opposed to short-term income fluctuations, is economic inactivity, which is unusually entrenched and concentrated in the UK, and affects children disproportionately. The reasons are to be found in the set-up of the welfare system. Empirically, wage elasticities of labour supply are highest among the low-skilled and especially single mothers. Ideally, marginal tax rates should be lowest on these groups. Yet the British welfare system has precisely the opposite effect. Through the interaction of taxation and benefit withdrawal, the weakest groups in the labour market are confronted with the highest implicit marginal tax rates. Uncertainty created by the benefit system's complexity exacerbates the problem. This monograph has proposed a breaking up of the multiple poverty traps through a drastic simplification and standardisation of the benefit system, the complete separation of benefit eligibility and tax liability, and a deep cut in effective marginal tax rates. Spending needs to be restrained, but there are better ways of achieving this than the imposition of high taper rates. An alternative would be to 'crowd in' rather than 'crowd out' the energy and efforts of the recipients. Instead of discouraging the recipients' own endeavours, a particular workload should be expected from them, as the very condition for the receipt of transfers. This would not only go with the grain of people's self-interest. It would also improve their social standing and self-esteem.

The quest to attain the previous, ill-defined poverty targets has failed. Both child poverty targets have been missed by a wide mark. A confused poverty strategy, torn between conflicting objectives, injected large amounts of public spending. But the strategy did not develop a dynamic of its own because it failed to unlock poor people's own potential for working towards the betterment of their position. Before rolling over the poverty targets to ever more distant future dates, the failure of the previous strategy should be reason to pause for thought. There is now an opportunity for rethinking what we really mean by poverty, and for re-evaluating the tools that work against it.

REFERENCES

Adam, S., M. Brewer and A. Shephard (2006), 'Financial work incentives in Britain: comparisons over time and between family types', Working Paper 06/2006, London: Institute for Fiscal Studies.

Alderson, A. and F. Nielsen (2002), 'Globalization and the great U-turn: inequality trends in 16 OECD countries', *American Journal of Sociology*, 107(5): 1244–99.

Andrews, K. and J. Jacobs (1990), *Punishing the Poor: Poverty under Thatcher*, London: Macmillan.

Anti Academies Alliance (n.d.), http://www.antiacademies.org. uk/, accessed May/June 2010.

Atkinson, A. (1998), *Poverty in Europe*, Oxford: Blackwell.

Attanasio, O., E. Battistin and A. Leicester (2006), 'From micro to macro, from poor to rich: consumption and income in the UK and the US', Paper prepared for the conference 'The Well Being of Families and Children as Measured by Consumption Behavior', National Poverty Center.

Barnardo's (2001), 'Action on child poverty must top the government's "to do" list, says Barnardo's', Press release, 8 June.

Baulch, B. (1996), 'The new poverty agenda: a disputed consensus', *IDS Bulletin*, 27(1), Institute of Development Studies.

BBC News (2006), 'Tories claim "big change" on poor', 24 November.

BBC World Service (2008), 'Widespread unease about economy and globalization', Global poll, 7 February.

Blackburn, M. (1998), 'The sensitivity of international poverty comparisons', *Review of Income and Wealth*, 44(4): 449–72.

Blanchflower, D. and A. Oswald (2004), 'Well-being over time in Britain and the USA', *Journal of Public Economics*, 88: 1359–86.

Blank, R. (1996), 'Why has economic growth been such an ineffective tool against poverty in recent years?', in J. Neill (ed.), *Poverty and Inequality. The Political Economy of Redistribution*, Kalamazoo, MI: Upjohn Institute.

Blank, R. and D. Card (1993), 'Poverty income distribution and growth: are they still connected?', Brookings Papers on Economic Activity, 2: 285–339.

Blow, L., A. Leicester and Z. Oldfield (2004), 'Consumption trends in the UK, 1975–99', London: Institute for Fiscal Studies.

Blundell, R. (2001), 'Welfare reform for low income workers', Oxford Economic Papers, 53/2001, pp. 189–214.

Blundell, R., A. Duncan and C. Meghir (1998), 'Estimating labor supply responses using tax reforms', *Econometrica*, 66(4): 827–61.

Blundell, R. and B. Etheridge (2008), 'Consumption, income and earnings inequality in the UK', London: Institute for Fiscal Studies and University College London.

Boarini, R. and M. d'Ercole (2006), 'Measures of material deprivation in OECD countries', OECD Social, Migration and Employment Working Papers, 37, OECD.

Booth, P. (2008), 'The young held to ransom – a public choice analysis of the UK state pension system', *Economic Affairs*, 28(1): 4–10.

Bradshaw, J. and N. Finch (2003), 'Overlaps in dimensions of poverty', *Journal of Social Policy*, 32(4): 513–25.

Brady, D. (2003a), 'Rethinking the sociological measurement of poverty', *Social Forces*, 81(3): 715–52.

Brady, D. (2003b), 'The politics of poverty: left political institutions, the welfare state, and poverty', *Social Forces*, 82(2): 557–88.

Brewer, M. (2009), 'How do income support systems in the UK affect labour force participation?', Working Paper 2009: 27, Institute for Labour Market Policy Evaluation.

Brewer, M. and J. Browne (2006), 'The effect of the Working Families' Tax Credit on labour market participation', IFS Briefing Note no. 69, London: Institute for Fiscal Studies.

Brewer, M. and A. Shephard (2004), 'Has Labour made work pay?', London: Institute for Fiscal Studies and Joseph Rowntree Foundation.

Brewer, M., A. Goodman and A. Leicester (2006a), 'Household spending in Britain: what can it teach us about poverty?', London: Joseph Rowntree Foundation.

Brewer, M., A. Duncan, A. Shephard, M. Suarez and M. Jose (2006b), 'Did working families' tax credit work? The impact of in-work support on labour supply in Great Britain', *Labour Economics*, 13: 699–720.

Brewer, M., A. Muriel, D. Philips and L. Sibieta (2008a), 'Poverty and inequality in the UK 2008', IFS Commentary 105, London: Institute for Fiscal Studies.

Brewer, M., E. Saz and A. Shephard (2008b), 'Means-testing and tax rates on earnings', Paper prepared for the Report of a Commission on Reforming the Tax System for the 21st century, chaired by Sir James Mirrlees ('Mirrlees Review'), London: Institute for Fiscal Studies.

Brewer, M., C. O'Dea, G. Paull and L. Sibieta (2009a), 'The living standards of families with children reporting low incomes', Research Report no. 577, London: Institute for Fiscal Studies, for the Department of Work and Pensions.

Brewer, M., A. Muriel and L. Wren-Lewis (2009b), 'Accounting for changes in inequality since 1968: decomposition analyses for Great Britain', London: Institute for Fiscal Studies, for the Government Equalities Office.

Browne, J. (2010), 'Taxing the rich: can it raise any money for the government?', *Economic Review*, 27(3).

Browning, E. (1989), 'Inequality and poverty', *Southern Economic Journal*, 55(4): 819–30.

Callan, T., B. Nolan and J. Walsh (1998), 'Income tax and social welfare policies', *Budget Perspectives*, Dublin: Economic and Social Research Institute.

Campaign for State Education (n.d.), http://www. campaignforstateeducation.org.uk/index.html, accessed May/June 2010.

Card, D. and J. DiNardo (2002), 'Skill-biased technological change and rising wage inequality: some problems and puzzles', NBER Working Paper 8769, Cambridge, MA: National Bureau of Economic Research.

Caritas Europa (2010), 'Poverty in Europe: background information and methods for youth'.

Caritas Switzerland (2010), *Sozialalmanach 2010. Schwerpunkt: Armut verhindern*, Luzern: Caritas-Verlag.

Central Intelligence Agency (CIA) (2009), *The World Factbook 2009*, Washington, DC: Central Intelligence Agency.

Central Statistics Office Ireland (2007), *Household Budget Survey 2004–2005. Final results*, Dublin: Stationery Office.

Child Poverty Action Group (2000), 'Tackling child poverty', CPAG Policy Briefing.

Child Poverty Action Group (2009), *Ending Child Poverty: a manifesto for success*, London: CPAG.

CIA World Factbook (2009), 'Country comparison: GDP per capita', https://www.cia.gov/library/publications/the-world-factbook/rankorder/2004rank.html.

Clark, A. and A. Oswald (1996), 'Satisfaction and comparison income', *Journal of Public Economics*, 61: 359–81.

Clark, J., G. Tullock and L. Levy (2006), 'The poverty of politics: how income redistribution hurts the poor', *Atlantic Economic Journal*, 34: 47–62.

Conservative Party (2008), 'Repair – our plan for social reform'.

Conservative Party (2010), 'Invitation to join the government of Britain. The Conservative Manifesto 2010'.

Coote, A., J. Franklin and A. Simms (2010), *21 Hours. Why a shorter working week can help us all to flourish in the 21st century*, London: New Economics Foundation.

Corkindale, J. (2004), *The Land Use Planning System*, London: Institute of Economic Affairs.

DeFina, R. (2002), 'The impact of macroeconomic performance on alternative poverty measures', *Social Science Research*, 31/2002, pp. 29–48.

Department for Environment, Food and Rural Affairs (2010), 'Data and resources: national indicators', http://www.defra.gov.uk/sustainable/government/progress/data-resources/national.htm.

Department for Work and Pensions (2010), *21st Century Welfare*, London: Stationery Office.

Dollar, D. and A. Kraay (2001), 'Growth is good for the poor', Policy Research Working Paper 2587, World Bank Development Research Group Macroeconomics and Growth.

Easterlin, R. (1995), 'Will raising the incomes of all increase the happiness of all?', *Journal of Economic Behavior and Organization*, 27: 35–47.

Easton, B. (2002), 'Beware the median', *SPRC Newsletter*, 82, November.

Eberstadt, N. (2007), 'Material deprivation, the "poverty rate" and household expenditure in modern America', *Economic Affairs*, 27(3): 15–23.

Economist (2010a), 'Whose backyard is it anyway?', 12 August.

Economist (2010b), 'First break all the rules', 15 April.

Edwards, C. and D. J. Mitchell (2008), *Global Tax Revolution. The Rise of Tax Competition and the Battle to Defend It*, Washington, DC: Cato Institute.

Einasto, M. (2002), 'Income and deprivation poverty, 1994 and 1999', in D. Kutsar (ed.), *Living Conditions in Estonia, Five Years Later*, Tartu: Tartu University.

End Child Poverty (n.d.), http://www.endchildpoverty.org.uk/.

Equality and Human Rights Commission (2009), 'Financial services enquiry. Sex discrimination and gender pay gap report of the Equality and Human Rights Commission'.

Esser, I. (2009), 'Has welfare made us lazy? Employment commitment in different welfare states', *British Social Attitudes*, 2008/2009, pp. 79–104, London: Sage Publications.

European Commission (1981), *Final Report from the Commission to the Council on the First Programme of Pilot Schemes and Studies to Combat Poverty*, Brussels: Commission of the European Communities.

European Commission (2004), *Joint Report on Social Inclusion*, Luxembourg: Office for Official Publications of the European Communities.

European Commission (2009), 'Literature review on the impact of family breakdown on children', Directorate-General for Employment, Social Affairs and Equal Opportunities, Unit for Social and Demographic Analysis.

Eurostat (2005a), 'Income poverty and social exclusion in the EU 25', *Statistics in Focus*, 13.

Eurostat (2005b), 'Material deprivation in the EU', *Statistics in Focus*, 21.

Eurostat (2006), 'Earnings disparities across European countries and regions. A glance at regional results of the Structure of Earnings Survey', *Statistics in Focus: Population and social conditions*, 7.

Eurostat (2008), 'The social situation in the European Union 2007. Social cohesion through equal opportunities', Luxembourg: Office for Official Publications of the European Communities.

Eurostat (2009a), 'What can be learned from material deprivation indicators in Europe', Methodologies and Working Papers, Luxembourg: Office for Official Publications of the European Communities.

Eurostat (2009b), *Labour Market Statistics*, Eurostat Pocket Books, Luxembourg: Publication Office of the European Union.

Eurostat (n.d.), online database, http://epp.eurostat.ec.europa. eu/portal/page/portal/statistics/themes.

Evans, A. and M. O. Hartwich (2005), *Unaffordable Housing, Fables and Myths*, London: Policy Exchange.

Evans, H. (2008), *Sixty Years On – Who Cares for the NHS?*, London: Institute of Economic Affairs.

Fafchamps, M. and F. Shilpi (2008), 'Subjective welfare, isolation, and relative consumption', *Journal of Development Economics*, 86: 43–60.

Falck, O., S. Heblich, A. Lameli and J. Suedekum (2010), 'Dialects, cultural identity, and economic exchange', IZA Discussion Paper no. 4743, Institute for the Study of Labour.

Fearon, D. (n.d.), 'Charles Booth: mapping London's poverty, 1885–1903', CSISS Classics, Center for Spatially Integrated Social Science.

Ferrer-i-Carbonell, A. (2005), 'Income and well-being: an empirical analysis of the comparison income effect', *Journal of Public Economics*, 89: 997–1019.

Forster, G. (2008), 'Vouchers and school choice: the evidence', *Economic Affairs*, 28(2): 42–7.

Förster, M. (1993), 'Comparing poverty in 13 OECD countries: traditional and synthetic approaches', Luxembourg Income Study Working Paper no. 100.

Frank, R. (1999), *Luxury Fever: Why Money Fails to Satisfy in an Era of Excess*, New York: Free Press.

Fraser Institute (2009), *Economic Freedom of the World. 2009 Annual Report*, Economic Freedom Network.

Friedman, M. (1957), *A Theory of the Consumption Function*, Princeton, NJ: Princeton University Press.

Fuchs, V. (1965), 'Towards a theory of poverty', in Chamber of Commerce of the United States of America, *Concept of Poverty*, Washington, DC: US Chamber of Commerce.

Galbraith, J. K. (1958), *The Affluent Society*, Boston, MA: Houghton Mifflin.

Gillie, A. (1996), 'The origin of the poverty line', *Economic History Review, New Series*, 49(4): 715–30.

Glennerster, H. (2004), 'The context for Rowntree's contribution', in H. Glennester, J. Hills, D. Piachaud and J. Webb (eds), *One Hundred Years of Poverty and Policy*, York: Joseph Rowntree Foundation.

Glynn, S. and A. Booth (1996), *Modern Britain: An economic and social history*, London and New York: Routledge.

Goodin, R. and J. Le Grand (1987), *Not Only the Poor: Middle Classes and the Welfare State*, London: Allen and Unwin.

Goodman, A. and S. Webb (1995), 'The distribution of UK household expenditure, 1979–92', London: Institute for Fiscal Studies.

Gordon, D. (2006), 'The concept and measurement of poverty', in C. Patanzis, D. Gordon and R. Levithas (eds), *Poverty and Social Exclusion in Britain*, Bristol: Policy Press.

Gordon, D., R. Levitas, C. Patanzis, D. Patsios, S. Payne, P. Townsend, L. Adelman, K. Ashworth, S. Middleton, J.

Bradshaw and J. Williams (2000), *Poverty and Social Exclusion in Britain*, York: Joseph Rowntree Foundation.

Green, K. (2009), 'To tackle child poverty we must also address inequality', Touchstone blog, Trade Union Congress, 25 November.

Greenberg, D., D. Linksz and M. Mandell (2003), *Social Experimentation and Public Policymaking*, Washington, DC: Urban Institute Press.

Gregg, P., S. Harkness and S. Machin (1999), 'Child poverty and its consequences', Ref. 389, London: Joseph Rowntree Foundation.

Guardian (2009), 'Majority of children living in poverty have at least one parent in work, says study', 18 February.

Guardian (2010), 'Does getting tough on the unemployed work?', 16 June.

Guio, A., A. Fusco and E. Marlier (2009), 'A European Union approach to material deprivation using EU-SILC and Eurobarometer data', Integrated Research Infrastructure in the Socio-economic Sciences (IRISS) Working Paper Series 19/2009, *International Networks for Studies in Technology, Environment, Alternatives and Development*.

Harberger, A. (1998), 'Monetary and fiscal policy for equitable economic growth', in V. Tanzio and Ke-young Chu (eds), *Income Distribution and High-Quality Growth*, Cambridge, MA: MIT, pp. 203–42.

Hatfield, M. (2002), 'Constructing the revised Market Based Measure', Applied Research Branch, Strategic Policy, Human Resources Development Canada.

Hatton, T. and R. Bailey (2000), 'Seebohm Rowntree and the post-war poverty puzzle', CEPR Discussion Paper no. 2147, London: Centre for Economic Policy Research.

Heath, A. (2006), *The Flat Tax: Towards a British model*, London: Taxpayers' Alliance.

Heritage Foundation (2010), *2010 Index of Economic Freedom*, Washington, DC: Heritage Foundation.

Hills, J. (2004), *Inequality and the State*, Oxford: Oxford University Press.

HM Treasury (2000), 'Tackling poverty and making work pay: tax credits for the 21st century', *The Modernisation of Britain's Tax and Benefit System*, 6, London: HM Treasury.

HM Treasury, Department for Children, Schools and Families & Department for Work and Pensions (2010), 'Ending child poverty: mapping the route to 2020', Strategic Direction Paper.

Horton, T. and J. Gregory (2009), *The Solidarity Society*, London: Fabian Society.

House of Commons (1990), Hansard Debates for 22 November, col. 448, http://www.publications.parliament.uk/pa/cm199091/cmhansrd/1990–11–22/Debate-3.html.

Human Resources and Social Development Canada (2008), *Low Income in Canada 2000–2004: Using the Market Basket Measure*.

Hunt, J. and G. Clark (2007), *Who's Progressive Now?*, London: Conservative Party.

Hunt, L. (ed.) (2003), *Energy in a Competitive Market. Essays in Honour of Colin Robinson*, Cheltenham: Edward Elgar.

Institute for Fiscal Studies (2007), 'Poverty and inequality', Presentation by A. Muriel.

Institute for Fiscal Studies (2008), 'Poorest households face highest average inflation rates', Press release, 14 October.

Institute for Fiscal Studies (2009), 'Average inflation falls, but remains high for some', IFS Press release, 9 March.

Institute for Fiscal Studies (2010), Inequality and Poverty spreadsheet, online spreadsheet accompanying 'Poverty and inequality in the UK: 2010', *IFS Commentary*, 116.

Institute for Public Policy Research (2009), 'Nice work if you can get it. Achieving a sustainable solution to low pay and in-work poverty'.

Ipsos MORI (2006), 'Over one in ten Londoners say they are living below the poverty line', Poll for the Church Urban Fund, 5 June.

Johns, H. and P. Ormerod (2007), *Happiness, Economics and Public Policy*, London: Institute of Economic Affairs.

Jones, C. and T. Novak (1999), *Poverty, Welfare and the Disciplinary State*, London and New York: Routledge.

Joseph Rowntree Foundation (2010), 'A minimum income standard for the UK in 2010', York: JRF.

Joyce, R., A. Muriel, D. Phillips and L. Sibieta (2010), *Poverty and Inequality in the UK: 2010*, London: Institute for Fiscal Studies.

Kangas, O. and R. Ritakallio (2004), 'Relative to what? Cross-national picture of European poverty measured by regional, national and European standards', Working Paper no. 384, Luxembourg Income Study Working Paper Series.

Karelis, C. (2007), *The Persistence of Poverty. Why the Economics of the Well-Off Can't Help the Poor*, New Haven, CT, and London: Yale University Press.

Kastendiek, H. (1999), *Grossbritannien – ein Erfolgsmodell?: Die*

Modernisierung unter Thatcher und New Labour, Bonn: Friedrich Ebert Stiftung.

Kay, L. (2010), 'Escaping the poverty trap: helping people on benefits into work', Policy Exchange.

Kelly, G. (1999), 'Is Thatcherism dead?', BBC News, Special report: Thatcher Anniversary.

Kenworthy, L. (1998), 'Do social-welfare policies reduce poverty? A cross-national assessment', Working Paper no. 188, Luxembourg Income Study.

Kenworthy, L., J. Epstein and D. Duerr (2009), 'Growth, redistribution and poverty', Working Paper, Department of Sociology, University of Arizona.

Kim, H. (2000), 'Anti-poverty effectiveness of taxes and income transfers in welfare states', *International Social Security Review*, 53(4): 105–29.

Korpi, W. and J. Palme (1998), 'The paradox of redistribution and strategies of equality: welfare institutions, inequality and poverty in the Western countries', *American Sociological Review*, 63: 661–87.

Krueger, A. and B. Meyer (2002), 'Labour supply effects of social insurance', in A. Auerbach and M. Feldstein (eds), *Handbook of Public Economics*, 1st edn, vol. 4, Amsterdam: Elsevier, pp. 2327–92.

Kuhn, P., P. Kooreman, A. Soetevent and A. Kapteyn (2008), 'The own and social effects of an unexpected income shock: evidence from the Dutch Postcode Lottery', Working Paper WR-574, RAND Labour and Population.

Labour Party (2010), 'A future fair for all. The Labour Party manifesto 2010'.

Lane, R. (1993), 'Does money buy happiness?', *The Public Interest*, 113/1993, pp. 56–65.

Lawlor, E., A. Kersley and S. Steed (2009), 'A bit rich: calculating the real value to society of different professions', London: New Economics Foundation.

Layard, R. (2005), 'Happiness is back', *Prospect*, 108/2005, pp. 14–21.

Leicester, A. (2006), 'Income and expenditure poverty', Presentation, London: Institute for Fiscal Studies.

Liberal Democrats (2007), 'Freedom from poverty, opportunity for all', Policy Paper 80.

Liberal Democrats (2010), 'Liberal Democrat manifesto 2010'.

Linsley, C. A. and C. L. Linsley (1993), 'Booth, Rowntree, and Llewelyn Smith: a reassessment of interwar poverty', *Economic History Review*, 46(1): 88–104.

Lohmann, H. (2006), 'Working poor in western Europe: what is the influence of the welfare state and labour market institutions?', Paper prepared for presentation at the 2006 Conference of the EuroPanel Users Network (EPUNet), 8/9 May, Barcelona.

Lomasky, L. and K. Swan (2009), 'Wealth and poverty in the liberal tradition', *Independent Review*, 13(4): 493–510.

Luttmer, E. (2004), 'Neighbors as negatives: relative earnings and well-being', Faculty Research Working Paper Series RWP 04–029, John F. Kennedy School of Government, Harvard University.

Madden, D. (2000), 'Relative or absolute poverty lines: a new approach', *Review of Income and Wealth*, 46(2): 181–99.

Maddison, A. (n.d.), 'Statistics on world population, GDP and per capita GDP, 1–2008 AD', dataset, http://www.ggdc.net/maddison/Historical_Statistics/horizontal-file_02–2010.xls.

Madrian, B. and D. Shea (2001), 'The power of suggestion: inertia in 401(k) participation and savings behaviour', *Quarterly Journal of Economics*, 116(4): 1149–87.

Marks, G. (2007), 'Income poverty, subjective poverty and financial stress', Social Policy Research Paper no. 29, Canberra: Australian Government Department of Families, Community Services and Indigenous Affairs.

Marr, A. (2007), *A History of Modern Britain*, London: Macmillan.

Martin, D. (2009), 'Benefit simplification: how, and why, it must be done', Centre for Policy Studies.

Marx, I. (2007), 'The Dutch miracle revisited: the impact of employment growth on poverty', *Journal of Social Policy*, 36(3): 383–97.

Matcovic, T., Z. Sucur and S. Zrinscak (2007), 'Inequality, poverty, and MD in new and old members of European Union', *Croatian Medical Journal*, 2007:48, pp. 636–52.

McBride, M. (2001), 'Relative-income effects on subjective well-being in the cross-section', *Journal of Economic Behavior and Organization*, 45: 251–78.

McKay, S. (2004), 'Poverty or preference: what do "consensual deprivation indicators" really measure?', *Fiscal Studies*, 25: 201–23.

Mead, L. (1999), 'The decline of welfare in Wisconsin', *Journal of Public Administration Research and Theory (J-PART)*, 9(4): 597–622.

Mead, L. (2004), *Government Matters. Welfare reform in Wisconsin*, Princeton, NJ: Princeton University Press.

Meghir, C. and D. Phillips (2008), 'Labour supply and taxes', Working Paper 08/04, London: Institute for Fiscal Studies.

Meyer, B. and J. Sullivan (2007), 'Three decades of consumption and income poverty', Harris School Working Paper Series 04.16, paper prepared for the Consumption, Income, and the Well-Being of Families and Children conference.

Michaud, S., C. Cotton and K. Bishop (2004), 'Exploration of methodological issues in the development of the market basket measure of low income for Human Resources Development Canada', Income Research Paper Series, Income Statistics Division, Statistics Canada.

Mitchel, D. (1991), *Income Transfers in Ten Welfare States*, Aldershot: Avebury.

Moller, S., M. Huber, J. Stephens, D. Bradley and F. Nielsen (2003), 'Determinants of RP in advanced capitalist democracies', *American Sociological Review*, 68(1): 22–51.

Morgan, P. (2007), *The War between the State and the Family. How Government Divides and Impoverishes*, London: Institute of Economic Affairs.

Muriel, A. (2008), 'Living standards and inequality', Presentation, London: Institute for Fiscal Studies, 11 June.

Muriel, A. and L. Sibieta (2009), 'Living standards during previous recessions', IFS Briefing Note BN85, London: Institute for Fiscal Studies.

Myck, M. (2005), 'How does material deprivation analysis fit into the theory of consumer choice?', Mimeo, Institute for Fiscal Studies.

Myddelton, D. R. (1994), *The Power to Destroy: An analysis of the British tax system*, London: Society for Individual Freedom.

Nardinelli, C. (n.d.), 'Industrial revolution and the standard of living', *The Concise Encyclopedia of Economics*, 2nd edn, Library of Economics and Liberty.

New Policy Institute & Joseph Rowntree Foundation (2007), *Monitoring Poverty and Social Exclusion 2007*, York: JRF.

New Policy Institute & Joseph Rowntree Foundation (n.d.), *The Poverty Site*, http://www.poverty.org.uk/.

Nielsen, L. (2009), 'Global relative poverty', IMF Working Paper 09/93, International Monetary Fund.

Niemietz, K. (2010a), 'Measuring poverty: context-specific but not relative', *Journal of Public Policy*, 30(3): 241–62.

Niemietz, K. (2010b), 'When paternalism meets bogus economics. The New Economics Foundation's *21 hours* report', IEA Current Controversies Paper no. 30, London: Institute of Economic Affairs.

Notten, G. and C. de Neubourg (2007), 'Relative or absolute poverty in the US and EU? The battle of the rates', MPRA Paper no. 5313, Munich Personal RePEc Archive.

OECD (2008), *Growing unequal? Income distribution and poverty in OECD countries*, Paris: OECD Publishing.

OECD (2009), *Education at a Glance 2009*, Paris: OECD Publishing.

OECD (2010), *Economic Policy Reforms: Going for growth*, Paris: OECD Publishing.

Office for National Statistics (2000), *Family Spending. A report on the 1999–2000 Family Expenditure Survey*, London: Stationery Office.

Office for National Statistics (2008), *Family Spending, 2007 edition*, Basingstoke: Palgrave Macmillan.

Office for National Statistics (2010a), *Family Spending. A report on the 2008 Living Costs and Food Survey*, Basingstoke: Palgrave Macmillan.

Office for National Statistics (2010b), Time series data, http://www.statistics.gov.uk/statbase/TSDSeries1.asp.

Office for National Statistics & Department for Work and Pensions (2009a), *Households below Average Income. An analysis of the income distribution 1994/95–2007/08*, London: ONS & DWP.

Office for National Statistics & Department for Work and Pensions (2009b), *Housing Benefit and Council Tax Benefit Summary Statistics*, http/asd/asd1/hb_ctb/index.php?page=hbctb_arc.

Office for National Statistics & HM Revenue and Customs (2009), 'Child and Working Tax Credits statistics: finalised annual awards 2007–08', London: ONS & HMRC.

Office for National Statistics & HM Revenue and Customs (2010), 'Child and Working Tax Credits statistics', London: ONS & HMRC.

Osamu, A. (2007), 'Perceptions of poverty in Japan: constructing an image of relative poverty contrasted against an image of extreme poverty', *Journal of Poverty*, 11(3): 5–14.

Oxfam Great Britain (n.d.), 'Resources: poverty in the UK', http://www.oxfam.org.uk/resources/ukpoverty/poverty_in_the_uk.html.

Oxford Economic Forecasting (2005), 'Trade liberalisation and CAP reform in the EU', OEF Report for Open Europe.

Pahl, R., D. Rose and L. Spencer (2007), 'Inequality and quiescence: a continuing conundrum', ISER Working Paper 2007–22, University of Essex.

Patanzis, C., D. Gordon and P. Townsend (2006), 'The necessities of life', in C. Patanzis, D. Gordon and R. Levithas (eds), *Poverty and Social Exclusion in Britain*, Bristol: Policy Press.

Pennington, M. (2002), *Liberating the Land: The Case for Private Land-Use Planning*, London: Institute of Economic Affairs.

Phillips, D. (2008), 'Living standards and poverty in the regions', Presentations, London: Institute for Fiscal Studies.

Pichaud, D. and J. Webb (2004), 'Why has poverty changed', in H. Glennester, J. Hills, D. Pichaud and J. Webb (eds), *One Hundred Years of Poverty and Policy*, York: Joseph Rowntree Foundation.

Picket, K. and R. Wilkinson (2007), 'Child wellbeing and income inequality in rich societies: ecological cross sectional study', *British Medical Journal*, 335: 1080–85.

Pissarides, C. (1992), 'Loss of skill during unemployment and the persistence of employment shocks', *Quarterly Journal of Economics*, 107: 1371–91.

Pryke, R. (1995), 'Taking the measure of poverty. A critique of low-income statistics: alternative estimates and policy implications', Research Monograph 51, London: Institute of Economic Affairs.

Rainwater, L., T. Smeeding and J. Coder (2003), 'Poverty across states, nations and continents', in K. Vleminckx and T. Smeeding (eds), *Child Well-being, Child Poverty and Child Policy in Modern Nations: What do we know?*, Bristol: Policy Press, pp. 33–74.

Ravallion, M. and S. Chen (2009), 'Weakly relative poverty', Policy Research Working Paper 4844, Development Research Group, World Bank.

Ravallion, M., D. Gaurav and D. v. d. Walle (1991), 'Quantifying absolute poverty in the developing world', *Review of Income and Wealth*, 37: 345–61.

Robinson, C. (ed.) (2001), *Regulating Utilities: New Issues, New Solutions*, Cheltenham: Edward Elgar.

Rowntree, S. B. (1922), *Social Theories of the City*, London: Routledge/Thoemmes Press (reprinted 1997).

Runciman, W. G. (1966), *Relative Deprivation and Social Justice*, London: Routledge & Kegan Paul.

Sarlo, C. (2007), 'Measuring poverty – what happened to Copenhagen?', *Economic Affairs*, 27(3): 6–14.

Sarlo, C. (2008), 'What is poverty? Providing clarity for Canada', Digital publication, Fraser Institute.

Saunders, P. (2001), 'Australia is not Sweden. National cultures and the welfare state', *Policy*, 17(3): 29–32.

Saunders, P. (2009), 'Poverty of ambition: why we need a new approach to tackling child poverty', Research Note, Policy Exchange.

Saunders P. and T. Smeeding (2002), 'Beware the mean!', *SPRC Newsletter*, 81, May.

Save the Children (2000), 'What is child poverty? Facts, measurements, and conclusions'.

Save the Children (2010), 'Measuring severe child poverty in the UK', Policy briefing.

Save the Children (n.d.), http://www.savethechildren.org.uk/.

Schneider, F. (2006), 'Shadow economies and corruption all over the world: what do we really know?', IZA Discussion Paper no. 2315, Institute for the Study of Labor.

Scruggs, L. and J. Allan (2006), 'The material consequences of welfare states. Benefit generosity and AP in 16 OECD countries', *Comparative Political Studies*, 39(7): 880–904.

Sefton, T. (2009), 'Moving in the right direction? Public attitudes to poverty, inequality and redistribution', in J. Hills, T. Sefton and K. Stewart (eds), *Towards a More Equal Society? Poverty, inequality and policy since 1997*, Bristol: Policy Press.

Sefton, T., J. Hills and H. Sutherland (2009), 'Poverty, inequality and redistribution', in J. Hills, T. Sefton and K. Stewart (eds), *Towards a More Equal Society? Poverty, inequality and policy since 1997*, Bristol: Policy Press.

Sen, A. (1976), 'Poverty: an ordinal approach to measurement', *Econometrica*, 44(2): 219–31.

Sen, A. (1983), 'Poor, relatively speaking', *Oxford Economic Papers, New Series*, 35(2): 153–69.

Sen, A. (2006), 'Conceptualizing and measuring poverty', in D. Grusky and R. Kanbur (eds), *Poverty and Inequality*, Stanford, CA: Stanford University Press, pp. 30–46.

Simms, A., V. Johnson and P. Chowla (2010), *Growth Isn't Possible. Why we need a new economic direction*, London: New Economics Foundation.

Smeeding, T. (2006), 'Poor people in rich nations. The United States in comparative perspective', *Journal of Economic Perspectives*, 20(1): 69–90.

Smith, D. (2006), *Living with Leviathan. Public Spending, Taxes and Economic Performance*, London: Institute of Economic Affairs.

Stevenson, B. and J. Wolfers (2008), 'Economic growth and subjective well-being: reassessing the Easterlin Paradox', IZA Discussion Paper no. 3654, Forschungsinstitut zur Zukunft der Arbeit.

Stewart, K., T. Sefton and J. Hills (2009), 'Introduction', in J. Hills, T. Sefton and K. Stewart (eds), *Towards a More Equal Society? Poverty, inequality and policy since 1997*, Bristol: Policy Press.

Sutherland, H., T. Sefton and D. Pichaud (2003), *Poverty in Britain. The impact of government policy since 1997*, London: Joseph Rowntree Foundation.

Townsend, P. (1954), 'Measuring poverty', *British Journal of Sociology*, 5(2): 130–37.

Townsend, P. (1962), 'The meaning of poverty', *British Journal of Sociology*, 13(3): 210–27.

Townsend, P. (1979), *Poverty in the United Kingdom. A survey of household resources and standards of living*, Berkeley and Los Angeles: University of California Press.

Townsend, P. (1980), 'Research on poverty', in A. Atkinson (ed.), *Wealth, Income and Inequality*, Oxford: Oxford University Press, pp. 299–306.

Toynbee, P. (2008), 'Unjust rewards', *Poverty*, 131: 6–8.

Trabandt, M. and H. Uhlig (2009), 'How far are we from the slippery slope? The Laffer Curve revisited', NBER Working Paper no. 15343, National Bureau of Economic Research.

Tullock, G. (1976), *The Vote Motive*, Hobart Paperback 9, London: Institute of Economic Affairs.

UNICEF Innocenti Research Center (2005), 'Child poverty in rich countries', Innocenti Report Card 6, Florence: UNICEF.

UNICEF Innocenti Research Center (2007), 'Child poverty in perspective: an overview of child well-being in rich countries', Innocenti Report Card 7, Florence: UNICEF.

United Nations Development Programme (2009), 'Indicators – Human Development Report 2009', online database, http:// hdrstats.undp.org/en/indicators/.

Van de Stadt, H., A. Kapteyn and S. van de Geer (1985), 'The relativity of utility: evidence from panel data', *Review of Economics and Statistics*, 67(2): 179–87.

Van den Bosch, K., T. Callan, J. Estivill, P. Hausman, B. Jeandidier, R. Muffels and J. Yfantopoulos (1993), 'A comparison of poverty in seven European countries and regions using subjective and relative measures', *Journal of Population Economics*, 6(3): 235–59.

Wilkinson, R. and K. Pickett (2009), *The Spirit Level. Why More Equal Societies Almost Always Do Better*, London: Penguin.

Wilkinson, R. and K. Pickett (2010), Presentation to the Royal Society for the Encouragement of Arts, Manufactures and Commerce (RSA), July, http://www.thersa.org/events/ audio-and-past-events/2010/the-spirit-level.

Wilkinson, W. (2009), 'Thinking clearly about economic inequality', Policy Analysis no. 640, Washington, DC: Cato Institute.

Wolff, E. (2009), *Poverty and Income Distribution*, 2nd edn, Wiley Blackwell.

Woodward, D. and A. Simms (2006), *Growth Isn't Working. The unbalanced distribution of benefits and costs from economic growth*, London: New Economics Foundation.

World Bank (2005), *An Introduction to Poverty Analysis*, Washington, DC: World Bank Institute.

World Bank (2006), *World Development Indicators*, Table 2.7, Washington, DC: World Bank.

ABOUT THE IEA

The Institute is a research and educational charity (No. CC 235 351), limited by guarantee. Its mission is to improve understanding of the fundamental institutions of a free society by analysing and expounding the role of markets in solving economic and social problems.

The IEA achieves its mission by:

- a high-quality publishing programme
- conferences, seminars, lectures and other events
- outreach to school and college students
- brokering media introductions and appearances

The IEA, which was established in 1955 by the late Sir Antony Fisher, is an educational charity, not a political organisation. It is independent of any political party or group and does not carry on activities intended to affect support for any political party or candidate in any election or referendum, or at any other time. It is financed by sales of publications, conference fees and voluntary donations.

In addition to its main series of publications the IEA also publishes a quarterly journal, *Economic Affairs*.

The IEA is aided in its work by a distinguished international Academic Advisory Council and an eminent panel of Honorary Fellows. Together with other academics, they review prospective IEA publications, their comments being passed on anonymously to authors. All IEA papers are therefore subject to the same rigorous independent refereeing process as used by leading academic journals.

IEA publications enjoy widespread classroom use and course adoptions in schools and universities. They are also sold throughout the world and often translated/reprinted.

Since 1974 the IEA has helped to create a worldwide network of 100 similar institutions in over 70 countries. They are all independent but share the IEA's mission.

Views expressed in the IEA's publications are those of the authors, not those of the Institute (which has no corporate view), its Managing Trustees, Academic Advisory Council members or senior staff.

Members of the Institute's Academic Advisory Council, Honorary Fellows, Trustees and Staff are listed on the following page.

The Institute gratefully acknowledges financial support for its publications programme and other work from a generous benefaction by the late Alec and Beryl Warren.

The Institute of Economic Affairs
2 Lord North Street, Westminster, London SW1P 3LB
Tel: 020 7799 8900
Fax: 020 7799 2137
Email: iea@iea.org.uk
Internet: iea.org.uk

Other papers recently published by the IEA include:

Towards a Liberal Utopia?
Edited by Philip Booth
Hobart Paperback 32; ISBN 0 255 36563 2; £15.00

The Way Out of the Pensions Quagmire
Philip Booth & Deborah Cooper
Research Monograph 60; ISBN 0 255 36517 9; £12.50

Black Wednesday
A Re-examination of Britain's Experience in the Exchange Rate Mechanism
Alan Budd
Occasional Paper 135; ISBN 0 255 36566 7; £7.50

Crime: Economic Incentives and Social Networks
Paul Ormerod
Hobart Paper 151; ISBN 0 255 36554 3; £10.00

The Road to Serfdom *with* **The Intellectuals and Socialism**
Friedrich A. Hayek
Occasional Paper 136; ISBN 0 255 36576 4; £10.00

Money and Asset Prices in Boom and Bust
Tim Congdon
Hobart Paper 152; ISBN 0 255 36570 5; £10.00

The Dangers of Bus Re-regulation
and Other Perspectives on Markets in Transport
John Hibbs et al.
Occasional Paper 137; ISBN 0 255 36572 1; £10.00

The New Rural Economy
Change, Dynamism and Government Policy
Berkeley Hill et al.
Occasional Paper 138; ISBN 0 255 36546 2; £15.00

The Benefits of Tax Competition
Richard Teather
Hobart Paper 153; ISBN 0 255 36569 1; £12.50

Wheels of Fortune
Self-funding Infrastructure and the Free Market Case for a Land Tax
Fred Harrison
Hobart Paper 154; ISBN 0 255 36589 6; £12.50

Were 364 Economists All Wrong?
Edited by Philip Booth
Readings 60; ISBN 978 0 255 36588 8; £10.00

Europe After the 'No' Votes
Mapping a New Economic Path
Patrick A. Messerlin
Occasional Paper 139; ISBN 978 0 255 36580 2; £10.00

The Railways, the Market and the Government
John Hibbs et al.
Readings 61; ISBN 978 0 255 36567 3; £12.50

Corruption: The World's Big C
Cases, Causes, Consequences, Cures
Ian Senior
Research Monograph 61; ISBN 978 0 255 36571 0; £12.50

Choice and the End of Social Housing
Peter King
Hobart Paper 155; ISBN 978 0 255 36568 0; £10.00

Sir Humphrey's Legacy
Facing Up to the Cost of Public Sector Pensions
Neil Record
Hobart Paper 156; ISBN 978 0 255 36578 9; £10.00

The Economics of Law
Cento Veljanovski
Second edition
Hobart Paper 157; ISBN 978 0 255 36561 1; £12.50

Living with Leviathan
Public Spending, Taxes and Economic Performance
David B. Smith
Hobart Paper 158; ISBN 978 0 255 36579 6; £12.50

The Vote Motive
Gordon Tullock
New edition
Hobart Paperback 33; ISBN 978 0 255 36577 2; £10.00

Waging the War of Ideas
John Blundell
Third edition
Occasional Paper 131; ISBN 978 0 255 36606 9; £12.50

The War Between the State and the Family
How Government Divides and Impoverishes
Patricia Morgan
Hobart Paper 159; ISBN 978 0 255 36596 3; £10.00

Capitalism – A Condensed Version
Arthur Seldon
Occasional Paper 140; ISBN 978 0 255 36598 7; £7.50

Catholic Social Teaching and the Market Economy
Edited by Philip Booth
Hobart Paperback 34; ISBN 978 0 255 36581 9; £15.00

Adam Smith – A Primer
Eamonn Butler
Occasional Paper 141; ISBN 978 0 255 36608 3; £7.50

Happiness, Economics and Public Policy
Helen Johns & Paul Ormerod
Research Monograph 62; ISBN 978 0 255 36600 7; £10.00

They Meant Well
Government Project Disasters
D. R. Myddelton
Hobart Paper 160; ISBN 978 0 255 36601 4; £12.50

Rescuing Social Capital from Social Democracy
John Meadowcroft & Mark Pennington
Hobart Paper 161; ISBN 978 0 255 36592 5; £10.00

Paths to Property
Approaches to Institutional Change in International Development
Karol Boudreaux & Paul Dragos Aligica
Hobart Paper 162; ISBN 978 0 255 36582 6; £10.00

Prohibitions
Edited by John Meadowcroft
Hobart Paperback 35; ISBN 978 0 255 36585 7; £15.00

Trade Policy, New Century
The WTO, FTAs and Asia Rising
Razeen Sally
Hobart Paper 163; ISBN 978 0 255 36544 4; £12.50

Sixty Years On – Who Cares for the NHS?
Helen Evans
Research Monograph 63; ISBN 978 0 255 36611 3; £10.00

Taming Leviathan
Waging the War of Ideas Around the World
Edited by Colleen Dyble
Occasional Paper 142; ISBN 978 0 255 36607 6; £12.50

The Legal Foundations of Free Markets
Edited by Stephen F. Copp
Hobart Paperback 36; ISBN 978 0 255 36591 8; £15.00

Climate Change Policy: Challenging the Activists
Edited by Colin Robinson
Readings 62; ISBN 978 0 255 36595 6; £10.00

Should We Mind the Gap?
Gender Pay Differentials and Public Policy
J. R. Shackleton
Hobart Paper 164; ISBN 978 0 255 36604 5; £10.00

Pension Provision: Government Failure Around the World
Edited by Philip Booth et al.
Readings 63; ISBN 978 0 255 36602 1; £15.00

New Europe's Old Regions
Piotr Zientara
Hobart Paper 165; ISBN 978 0 255 36617 5; £12.50

Central Banking in a Free Society
Tim Congdon
Hobart Paper 166; ISBN 978 0 255 36623 6; £12.50

Verdict on the Crash: Causes and Policy Implications
Edited by Philip Booth
Hobart Paperback 37; ISBN 978 0 255 36635 9; £12.50

The European Institutions as an Interest Group
The Dynamics of Ever-Closer Union
Roland Vaubel
Hobart Paper 167; ISBN 978 0 255 36634 2; £10.00

An Adult Approach to Education
Alison Wolf
Hobart Paper 168; ISBN 978 0 255 36586 4; £10.00

Other IEA publications

Comprehensive information on other publications and the wider work of the IEA can be found at www.iea.org.uk. To order any publication please see below.

Personal customers

Orders from personal customers should be directed to the IEA:
Sam Collins
IEA
2 Lord North Street
FREEPOST LON10168
London SW1P 3YZ
Tel: 020 7799 8907. Fax: 020 7799 2137
Email: scollins@iea.org.uk

Trade customers

All orders from the book trade should be directed to the IEA's distributor:
Gazelle Book Services Ltd (IEA Orders)
FREEPOST RLYS-EAHU-YSCZ
White Cross Mills
Hightown
Lancaster LA1 4XS
Tel: 01524 68765. Fax: 01524 53232
Email: sales@gazellebooks.co.uk

IEA subscriptions

The IEA also offers a subscription service to its publications. For a single annual payment (currently £42.00 in the UK), subscribers receive every monograph the IEA publishes. For more information please contact:
Sam Collins
Subscriptions
IEA
2 Lord North Street
FREEPOST LON10168
London SW1P 3YZ
Tel: 020 7799 8907. Fax: 020 7799 2137
Email: scollins@iea.org.uk